Wishing you the best
Eldon Hostetler

The Life and Times of …

Eldon "Ziggity" Hostetler

An Autobiography

Eldon "Ziggity" Hostetler

Published by LaGwana Printing, Inc.
Indiana, USA - Copyright 2008

Table of Contents

Chapter 1

The History of Eldon Hostetler

I was born on the Pashan farm, the oldest of thirteen children, nine girls and four boys, to parents Mahlon and Lizzie (Schrock) Hostetler. Three of the sisters and one brother are now deceased.

Name	Date of Birth	
Eldon	December 25, 1922	
Ida Mae	July 26, 1924	
David	January 4, 1926	died November 20, 2001
Anna	September 9, 1927	died March 14, 2004
Nina	November 22, 1931	died January 29, 1932
Orpha	June 20, 1933	
Mary Etta	June 4, 1935	
Mabel Irene	July 20, 1937	died October 14, 2002
Elizabeth Ann	July 12, 1939	
Freida Marie	March 9, 1942	
Leah Fern	May 17, 1945	
Daniel	June 8, 1949	
LaVern	May 16, 1952	

(Left) My mother, Lizzie (Schrock) Hostetler, with a granddaughter.
(Above) My father, Mahlon Hostetler.

Pashan Farm, near Shipshewana, Indiana, where I grew up.

My parents owned what was known as the Pashan Farm. My mother was a daughter of David and Anna (Bontrager) Schrock, who lived next door to us. David Schrock became quite an influence in my life; I'll touch on that later. Although Mahlon and Lizzie were Old Order Amish, Jacob P. Miller, a Mennonite bishop from Shore Church, married them. In those days, the Amish did not follow the wedding ritual that is normally used now.

Pashan was considered a town before Shipshewana was. Back in the 1880s, the Pashan Farm was a store. It was located on the east side of what is now County Road 1000W, about half a mile south of US 20. When I was a child, my grandmother would tell me that she used to walk about two miles through the woods to go to the Pashan store to buy general merchandise and do her shopping. That store — the building in which I was born and which later became a home — was filled with general merchandise of all kinds. A doctor's office and a post office occupied space there, as well as an attached home for the curator or keeper of the store. Across the street were four lots. Two of the lots were used for our truck patch, and the other two lots had homes on them. A sawmill and a blacksmith shop also operated at that location. When the railroad came through Shipshewana, the post office was moved there.

Dad was a farmer by trade and originally farmed eighty acres. Grandpa Schrock, who was a thresher by trade, lived about 500 feet south of our farm. I was more interested in what Grandpa Schrock was doing than I was in farming, but I did put effort into helping Dad. Whenever I could, I also helped Grandpa. Grandpa had us farm his eighty acres, and Dad bought sixty acres at the back end of our farm, added it to ours, and that made ours one hundred and forty acres. Then he bought fifty acres on the north side of US 20, about a mile away from where we lived, and Grandpa Schrock had ten acres up on highway US 20.

A lot of work needed to be done and, at an early age, I was expected to help.

One of my earliest remembrances of things that happened in my life that I might share is that my Dad was an individual who had a way of expressing himself in what he said and what he did that left a lasting impression. One of those was that when I was a very young child, he would take me along to the Shipshe sale once in a while. One time, when he didn't plan to take me, I threw myself face down on the ground, kicking and screaming, wanting to go along. When I wasn't looking, he went over to the stock tank, filled a five-gallon bucket, and gave me a bath. That is something I'll never forget because he didn't have to say a word. I got up and ran for the house, where Mother had to get me some dry clothes. That was my last tantrum. Although that is one of my earliest recollections and seems kind of funny now, it taught me a lasting lesson. Dad taught me many others, which I'll share as I go along.

Another thing I remember was that my grandfather, as a very young man, had a steam engine for threshing, and he decided to take it to Goshen and trade it for a 20-40 Huber tractor. One morning I got up early and watched as the tractor, which was a steam engine, left for Goshen for the last time. Later in the day, my dad took me in the buggy to Goshen, and I was privileged to drive back with Grandpa on the 20-40 Huber tractor, which went about three times as fast as the steam engine would go in high gear. On the way back, we took County Road 22 and the Griner Road and stopped on the way to buy a spring wagon that he later converted to what we call an "oil wagon." He had a fifty-gallon drum with his fuel and oil and things on it, and he pulled it hundreds of miles around the country doing threshing.

Later, I did something which I'll share at this point because Grandpa was so influential in my life. It was very hard to start the tractor in the wintertime, so Grandpa had me go along with him in the fall of the year. We went down to the junk yard and found an old car. I don't remember whether it was a Buick or a Dodge, but it had what we referred to as a combination starter generator unit. The unit would act as a starter and then act as a generator after it was running. We took the car apart, took the flywheel off the car and the starter, brought it home, and then we mounted that thing inside the housing of the tractor. Finally, we put a starter button next to the seat of the tractor. Grandpa would get on the crank and I on the button, and between us, we could start that thing in zero weather, which was enough of a novelty that people from the factory came out to see the process. They had never heard of putting a starter in an old Huber tractor.

Life at our house continually had – how should I say it? – more excitement than most families experienced. We probably had more because of all the children and all the activities. Now that we are older, we enjoy thinking back on all the excitement. It made no difference whether it was raining, snowing, or whatever; we were always busy doing something. We were never allowed to just sit and think there was nothing to do because Dad always knew of something we could be doing. Because of that, I guess I grew up recognized by some as a workaholic. I don't know; that's a name that came into our vocabularies when people began talking about "taking a couple weeks of vacation," "having time off," and things like that. I remember my parents going on vacation only once in the twenty-one years I was at home with the family.

My dad always said I worked harder to make a project simple than I would if I were to just get to it and do it. That sometimes caused a few extra words of conversation about what were seen as my misplaced efforts to find a better way. For example, I used a litter carrier to take silage from the silo, which was on the west side of the barn, to the straw shed, which was on the east side of the barn. I put the silage in the litter carrier, pushed it out and dumped it in the straw shed in the feeding bunks for the cattle, instead of breaking my back carrying out the silage bushel after bushel in a basket. Getting that task accomplished was quite involved, but the method worked and was used many years after I left home. I guess the system was eventually dismantled. These are some of the little things I remember.

When we bought the sixty-acres at the back end of the farm, a big wood with lots of maple trees was included. We started tapping the trees in the spring of the year, gathering all the maple sap together, bringing it home, and taking it into the furnace house. We would take out three giant cast iron kettles, put on a big evaporator tray, start the fire, and begin boiling the sap water for maple syrup. We boiled as many as thirty or forty gallons of maple syrup each year. It takes thirty gallons of sap water to make a gallon of syrup. It was good to put on top of pancakes and bread, and we sold some of it. That was always an interesting spring job that I enjoyed. We would also soft boil eggs for breakfast in the sap water.

Our farm was cut up by branches of three open ditches. They joined and ran into one at Grandpa's farm. Muskrats and mink lived in the ditches. Fur from those animals was in demand, so when I was five years old, Dad showed me how to set traps to catch them. He gave me a flashlight to check the traps and bring home the horses. Instructions were: "Don't yell for help if you have a muskrat in the trap." Guess what? The first trap I came to had a muskrat splashing around, and the whole neighborhood knew I had caught a muskrat because of the way I hollered for Dad to come help remove it. During my time at home, I caught many dollars worth of mink and muskrats. One year I caught a very valuable white ermine.

When I was about six years old, a muskrat fell into one of our window wells. We had just filled the silo in the fall. Dad suggested we put the live muskrat into the silo and trap it after the season opened. Guess what? As we emptied the silo, the muskrat dug itself down, also. We never got to the muskrat until the silo was empty. We sure had a big fat muskrat. I'm certain Dad wouldn't recommend doing that again.

Rats were always scurrying around on the farm where we stored a lot of corn and such things. Dad gave us a nickel for every rat we caught and a penny for each mouse. He encouraged us to set traps. One time I saw a repeating rat trap on sale at the Shipshe Auction. It had a platform where the rats would get to the bait; a spring would trip them off the platform and throw them back into a receptacle where it would keep them.

The shop and the furnace room were joined. The floor in the shop was wood that was raised above the furnace floor level. That left dirt in both areas. The rats would dig holes in the dirt under the shop floor so I would crawl underneath the floor of the shop and set my traps. I caught quite a few. One day when I was just a young boy eight years old, I came back from school to find Dad had cemented the furnace area. I tried to push myself in to check the rat trap, but then I couldn't get back out because my head was caught. Dad had to go down to Grandpa's, borrow his big hydraulic jack, and jack the floor up in the shop so I could get my head out. I don't know what happened to the trap because I never got back to get it. I was unable to reach it after they raised the four inches of cement floor, and I couldn't crawl in anymore.

One other event that I get razzed about a lot, even in this day and age, happened on my grandpa's farm. He had a ten-acre field over on US 20, and he usually had corn planted there. As a young boy, my dad asked me to go along when they cut corn and put

(Left) The martin house I made for Ed Wolfe, and (Right) the wooden windmill I built for Mr. Yoder at Yoder Popcorn Company.

it in shocks. While they tied strings around the shocks so they wouldn't fall over, I was to carry the string bucket from one shock to the other. We took a real sharp straight knife along, and I was told not to play with it. Dad went down through the cornfield, making the saddles and getting ready to cut the corn. He put eighty hills of corn in a shock, and he'd cut a row down through and come back on the other side. A hired man helped him. He went down about five hundred feet and came back, and I was sitting there crying. Dad asked, "What happened?" I said, "I cut myself a long time ago, and it just started bleeding now." Of course, I was accused of trying to make an excuse out of something that wasn't true, so it turned into one of the little quips we sometimes get blessed with.

As a young boy, when I was about eight or nine years old, Ed Wolfe knew that I had put up a martin house at home. He asked me if I would build a martin house for him. I said I would. Of course, I had a whole collection of farm tools to work with! I had an old saw, a wood rasp, a hammer, a chisel, and brace and bits, and that was it! After a whole winter of night work, I finally finished by the time the martins arrived; Grandpa Schrock helped me put up the house at the Wolfe home. It was there for many years; I don't know whether it ever housed anything other than sparrows, but we mounted it right next to a building because the backyard really didn't give it much chance of working for martins. He paid me $25, and that was a lot of money back in those days. At the same time, I made a wooden windmill for Mr. Yoder at Yoder Popcorn Company. He kept it out in his front yard for many years. I made the windmill with a wheel that actually turned when the wind blew. It had a big shoe in the back for a vane, and I have an old picture of both the birdhouse and the windmill.

A couple of other things come to mind. On Sunday, my folks usually took time to sleep. One Sunday they were in bed sleeping, and they heard a buggy going by with its riders laughing loudly. They couldn't figure out what was happening, so they got up to see. I had made a singletree and a two-horse hitch and put ropes on it. I had hitched my brother David, my sister Ida, and myself on the handles of the garden-wheeled rake that we used to plow between rows of onions and different vegetables in the garden. We were out there plowing the garden — on a Sunday! — and my folks put a stop to that in a hurry. Those were some of the ways we generated our own excitement.

Another excitement that wasn't so delightful involved my dad who, for some reason, had a police dog. The police dog's name was Reeny. Dad had her tied up to a tree right next to the road. When I was about eight years old, I had David, my next younger brother, and Ida, my next younger sister, out in the wagon, and I hitched Reeny to the wagon. At first, that was no problem; she just pulled the wagon, and I led her. After a while, however, she got tired. She didn't want to play any longer; she just stood there. I told Ida to hold the dog while I went up to the granary and got a cat, knowing the dog was deadly on cats. I put the cat under my coat, walked out to the road and put Ida back in the wagon, took the strap I was using to lead the dog, and let the cat out of my coat. When the cat jumped, so did the dog, and so did David and Ida. The next thing I saw was a big cloud of dust going down the road as fast as the dog could go with the cat right in front of him. Grandpa's barn was about five hundred feet away, and the house was another hundred feet further. Beyond it was a chicken house, and under the chicken house was a place where the cat knew she was safe. She ran down the ditch on the west side of the road, and when the cat went across the road to get under the chicken house, the dog made a sharp turn, and guess what happened? David and Ida landed on the gravel road. They had a lot of gravel marks on their bodies. Other than that, they weren't hurt badly.

The dog jumped over the fence; the wagon was hanging on one side of the fence, and the dog was hanging on the other. I went to the side where the dog was, and he tried to bite me, but I couldn't get the straps loose from the wagon because they were pulled too tightly. A strap was on each side of the dog, and each ran back to the wagon handle. In those days, every kid had a pocketknife, so I took my knife from my pocket and cut both straps. After the dog hit the ground, he ran away and didn't come home for four days. When he finally came back, he was dragging two very short straps. I tried to persuade Dad I had chosen the only alternative open to me, but he never accepted that reasoning. It was the last punishment I remember that was meted out on my behind, but I guess I had it coming. That was another family experience that generated much conversation.

One other time, we went down to Grandpa's house. He had a lot of grain stored in his barn. In the spring, I was supposed to see to it that the windmill was turned on, and I forgot to do it. The girls decided that when we went down to clean oats at Grandpa's farm in the evening (we were going to plant oats the next day), they were going to watch the windmill until the tank was pumped full. David and I had been running the fanning mill and cleaning oats for seed when Dad decided we had done enough. We raced back to the house and came down over the bank around the barn. As we turned the corner, running and chasing each other and laughing, the girls suddenly jumped up. They had a blanket lying in front of the stock tank with a white duster covering their feet and bodies, and when we came, they didn't know whether it was a horse running or what! They jumped up with the white duster over themselves and with their legs flying. We made a U-turn, screamed, and ran for the house as fast as we could go because we didn't know what was happening. They thought it was so funny that they could scare us within an inch of our lives.

A couple of months later, we were still trying to think of a way to get even with the girls. We always had a brooder house with baby chicks in it, and it was set back in the orchard, which was north of the house and north of where the chickens were housed. We had to carry the chickens at night from the brooder house down to the laying house and clean it all up and get it ready for new pullets. I made it a point to get back in the orchard at night, and I made a sound like a bull that was really mad about something. The girls were carrying chickens. They dropped the chickens and ran as fast as they could for the house. That pretty much evened the score on that one.

Another memorable event happened when I was a little older. I was the oldest, and children didn't go to Communion at church when adults did. In order to entertain the rest of them, I decided to take a pair of Dad's underwear and the old Sears and Roebuck catalog. We ripped the pages out, stuffed the underwear full of the crinkled up paper, made a dummy by putting Dad's clothes on it (both his Sunday best and his work clothes), and doing different things with the dummy. Then we decided to get rid of the remaining paper. The round oak stove was usually used to heat the home during the winter. In the spring of year, Mother would take what was called "stove black" paint to coat the stovepipe because it always changed color during the times when it got quite hot. So, in order to make it look nice, she would paint the stove and the pipes black. The pipe went up into an elbow, then back toward the wall into another elbow, then up through the register into our bedroom, and then into another elbow into the chimney — three elbows. We decided to dump the papers into the stove. Guess what happened? When we lit the fire, it started to roar up through that pipe, and one thing Mother hadn't done was clean out the inside of the pipe. It had some kind of gunk stuck on the inside that caught fire, the stovepipe got red hot, and we didn't know what to do other than to pour water on it. When we did that, the black paint she had used started running down, and it made all kinds of marks on the floor. We didn't know what to do. We went outside and found the fire was coming out the top of the chimney about three feet high. Everything was on fire. When the door on the stove was closed, the stove would puff and blow the door open. We had put only about half the paper into the stove, yet it got so hot in the chimney that sparks showed up into the attic. We found the rafter that was right beside the chimney was on fire. I quickly ran out to the barn, got a syringe that my dad used to give medicine to the horses, and also took a bucket of water up to the attic. (We used to have water fights with those syringes, my brother and I.) We shot the water up between the rafter and the chimney. After a bit, the fire went down, and we got it out. By the time the folks came home, we had things somewhat cooled off and cleaned up. Mother cried, "Oh my goodness, what happened to the stove pipes?" We all stood there and looked at each other because we didn't know what to say. It didn't take them long to figure out what had happened. We had tried to burn paper in the stove, and we almost burned the house down.

Not long after that, Mother wanted to paper the girls' bedroom in another part of the house. A chimney stood in that room, and she thought she would take it down because it hadn't been used in years and years, and the bricks were coming apart. She started just tapping on the bricks, and they started coming out easily. I wasn't old enough, I guess, to understand that you don't take a chimney down from the bottom. But she did just that. She started throwing bricks out the window, and she had them all apart except the back side.

The back side was still there, and the bricks wouldn't budge because the weight of bricks went right on up and out through the roof. Now, Grandpa Schrock had what I would call a miniature sledgehammer with a short handle. I volunteered to run down to his place to get it. Grandmother showed me where it was, and I came back and gave it to Mother. She proceeded to hit the back bricks and, all of a sudden, they all came down. We had a whole room full of bricks right in the bedroom. That's a quick way to take a chimney down, but I wouldn't suggest it's the right way. That was another part of the excitement in our lives.

We had many apple trees that were used to make cider. A custom cider press was located nearby. Dad would have us help pick up apples, load them on the box wagon, and take them to the cider press. They would grind the apples and press the cider out of them. He would place a wood barrel with a spigot on it on the back of the spring wagon. We would go to Shipshewana Lake to sell fresh-made country cider to the people from Chicago. He had me drive the horse from home to home as he canvassed for sales. Many young boys and girls would follow him, because he gave them samples of the cider. Dad just loved to pick-up some scantily clad girl and seat her beside me to see how I would react. He did that to embarrass me, but that was Dad. Later, he would tease me about my reaction.

I haven't said much about my dad's parents who lived near Emmatown, Indiana. They were David and Leah (Lambright) Hostetler, and they came into the area when land was cheap and available. They purchased many acres that had muck land on them. Because of that, they grew a lot of mint, spearmint, and peppermint. During the war, those oils were used for medicinal purposes. They sold many dollars worth of spearmint. I helped weed and plant at a very young age. The muck ground was black and was mostly decayed grasses left by the glacier period. The dust from it made a person's whole body itch, and the only thing that stopped it was a bath.

My Grandpa had many acres of that kind of land and needed many helpers to keep out the weeds so it would qualify for medicinal use. When weeds were left in with the mint, certain kinds of weeds would contaminate the lot when it was distilled. Producing the product for the market required a very labor intensive program that involved many steps. First, the plants had to be pulled and placed in wooden crates and put in a ditch where water was deep enough to cover the roots. Many crates were filled after several days of picking; then it was time to plant. First, the two-row New Idea Mint Planter water tank was filled. Next, a team of slow walking horses was hitched to it. The plants in the stream were brought to the planter. Two people got into the location where they could place the plants about six inches apart in a planter row. The team driver had to keep the process going smoothly and control the water flow to the plants. Water was needed to get the plants started.

Soon after the rows of plants were completed, they grew bigger and so did the weeds.

That required that people go through the rows and pull out the weeds. When fall came, the plants were cut and left to dry some. Then, they were loaded on a wagon and taken to the mint still where they were put into a big diameter round tub that was six or more feet deep. When the tub was packed full, the lid was clamped down on it, and it was pressure sealed. Steam was turned onto the tub, and the oil was cooked out of the mint. The steam carried the oil with it to the condenser coils that had cold water flowing over them to separate the steam and oil. That was an extremely hot job, as was removing the hot distilled material from the tub, but it was what had to be done in order to get a field of mint started. The following year, when the mint was carpet type, the roots had runners that spread in all directions. Weeds competed with plants for growing space, so they needed to be removed before they got big. Carpet type mint lasted only a few years, and then the process started all over again. Grandma always had big dinner spreads for all the employees that were working for them.

My dad was born in a log house in a wood. He and his brother Owen slept in the loft. When Dad was about twelve years old, the family constructed a farm home out by the road on one of their land areas. Dad was born in 1900, which made it easy to remember his age. During my youth, Dad and I would go out in the coldest part of the winter to help harvest ice off Emma Lake. We would cut the ice in large blocks and lift it out onto farm wagons to store for later usage. Grandpa would use the old log home to store ice blocks in dust brought from the sawmill. We would put six inches of sawdust on the floor, stack blocks of ice on it eight inches apart, and then cover the blocks totally with six inches of sawdust. We would start another layer of ice blocks and cover them. That was done so they had ice to cool things in the summer. That way of packing made it possible to keep ice until August. We used to make our own ice cream during the hot summer months when there were no ice deliveries, refrigerators, or freezers in the country. The children helped each other with things that required manpower because there were no power units like the ones we have to do the job today.

When Dad was a young man, we went quite frequently to the Conservative Mennonite Church, then called the Town Line Church. That was in the late twenties, I guess '26 or '27. At that time, most members drove there with buggies, but some of them started buying cars. Mother wasn't very happy about that development. One day when I came back from the field with Dad, we saw that grandparents, David and Leah, were at the house. Dad put the teams away and came inside, also, and they all talked about a few things.

All of a sudden, the question of the reason for their visit came up. Dad said, "I probably know why you're here." Grandpa said, "Yeah, we heard that you made a down payment on buying a car." He asked Dad, "Is that true?"

Dad admitted he had put a $500 down payment on a 1929 Chrysler 75. Of course, Mother started crying. Grandpa said, "Well, if you're going to buy a car, I guess I'll have to disinherit you if you take delivery of it." Grandpa told Dad that if he would stay Amish, he would give him back the $500 if the dealer refused a refund. Dad sat there for a little bit, and he said, "Well, you know what the Bible says, '*The love of money is the root of all evil*'." Grandpa didn't say anything; he just sat there for a while.

Tears started running down the sides of his face. He got up, and the last thing he said as he walked out the door was that he loved my father and he hoped he wouldn't take delivery on the car. He reminded Dad of the vow he had made at baptism and added that he hoped he would stay in the faith. I guess it was at that time I realized how important vows are. Dad never got the car.

As a young child, that experience made an impression on my life that reached to my very soul. A lot of things had happened in those few moments, and many decisions had to be made. I realized how important it is that we make right decisions and that we make them at the right time.

At this point, it is probably good to talk a little bit about what the Amish really believe. I grew up that way, lived under that influence for twenty-one years, and my dad and mother and I had a lot of conversations about beliefs and the importance of certain beliefs. My mother was probably ten times stronger on living the Amish faith than my dad was because Dad thought of buying a car, and Mother was not too happy about that. She even knelt down beside the bed many days and prayed about that, and I stood or knelt there beside her as a young child and knew how she felt. Dad didn't think it was too important whether people were Mennonite, Amish Mennonite, or Amish.

The Amish operate under some rules that are very different from those of other churches. They have council meetings and communion twice a year. Each church is asked at each council meeting whether or not the members agree with the rules that were set forward during the previous year or the previous six months. At those meetings, everybody, both men and women, have the chance to express themselves on whether they agree completely with the rules and regulations.

For example, one church group might allow bicycles. Another church might not. Some churches might allow chain saws and another will not. These choices are all based on the individual church groups, so great differences can be found between them. I know the church I grew up in didn't allow bicycles.

At one time, my father received a tag with every bag of dairy supplement he bought to put with ground cow feed. He could rip the bottom off and put his name on it, and it would then be put in a drawing for different prizes. One year, the company was giving away a nice bicycle that was so rare that, if a person still owned it today, would be worth $6,000. I kept those tags as I opened the bags and mixed the supplement with the feed we were grinding. I signed my dad's name to them and put them into the box they were using to draw for different prizes at a meeting before Christmas. They would also have entertainment, which was usually some group that played guitars, accordions, banjos, and other instruments. At that particular one, I guess about 1936 or 1937, when the drawing was held, the name Mahlon Hostetler came up for the bicycle. And so, we had a bicycle, and I was elated. But it was at the next council meeting that it had already been determined that Dad could not own the bicycle. Dad came to me and said, "Well, the only thing I know is that if you want to have it, you can have it. I'll sell it to you for ten bucks." So I went down to the bank and drew ten dollars out of my savings. Such a withdrawal took that fund down considerably because, at five cents a piece for rats and what little other income I had, the savings hadn't built up very fast. But I owned a bicycle, and I kept that bicycle until I got a car. To this day, I don't know what I did with it; somehow, I can't remember whether I sold it or gave it to somebody. It's only been recently, in 2002, that the church I grew up in allowed bicycles and power-driven lawn mowers. Before that, the members had to use push-type lawn mowers to mow their lawns.

The Amish do have some very unusual ways of doing things, but it's a very democratic system. No committees are involved. Each person votes and, to me, this is quite unusual. Committees are involved in our church, and those committees decide what is to be done, and members had better shape up and go along with anything that is decided. That is different than the Amish way where one person can say he can't accept a certain thing or that he wants to do this and wants to do that, then the group has to go back and question each person about that subject. About ten years ago, if one of them said, "I want to have a bicycle for my sons. Why can't we have a bicycle? So-and-so church has bicycles, and we probably ought to put that on the agenda." In such cases, they would vote. If the majority says, "Yes, we should have bicycles," then, they have bicycles, but it has to be a majority. If somebody decides to get a bicycle after a negative vote, the elders will go out and visit him. If they decide he's not going to abide by the rules, he's not allowed to go along to communion. He is counseled from then on about his attitude. After three misses (three times, that's a year and a half), he is automatically expelled from the church. It won't make any difference if he buys a truck or decides to buy a tractor, which is something, but if he farms with it, that's not allowed. That may be an unusual way of doing things, but it promotes harmony within the church.

The Amish are a part of the Anabaptist faith, which started way back in Switzerland. As they came up across the plains in France, the Alsace Lorraine, they migrated, and when they were persecuted there, they kept moving. The name Anabaptist came about when Martin Luther first published the German translation of the Bible from Latin and everybody could read it and understand it. Some of them said, "Whoa, wait a minute. What the Catholics are promoting here is not quite factual. There's no reason to baptize these children because God doesn't hold people responsible until they come to the age of accountability." Now, during the time when the children of Israel were coming out of

Egypt and wandering through the desert (if you get your Bibles you can find it), we are told that anybody under twenty years of age was not held accountable when they got to the entrance to the Promised Land. Those people that were twenty years and younger could go in; they were not held accountable for anything that happened out there in the wilderness. Those older ones that did things and were involved in unacceptable things were not allowed to go in, including Moses himself. He wasn't allowed to go in because of some of the things he had done. And so, at practically every service every Sunday, the Amish start out with Genesis — why the world was formed and how it was formed and who formed it, and what man's relationship is to God. And that is always expounded upon. Some of them have different thoughts about some things, but what always intrigues me is that a minister may come from a different church, and although he may have had different rules and regulations in his district, the people don't expect a visiting preacher to talk about those differences. He will talk about Jesus Christ and Him crucified and resurrected. Of course, he will start out with the Old Testament and go through all those things, and then he'll get into the New Testament; that's why it takes three hours for them to have a regular service. They touch upon all the high points.

I could pretty much tell you the outline of every Amish service, even in this day and age, just remembering what happened when I was living at home. I'm past eighty years old today. I have sisters still living, and they have daughters getting married as well as children that have passed away. When my sisters passed away, I was at those services, I understood the services, and I knew what they were saying because everything is taught and spoken in the old Martin Luther German or what they call the Plautdietsch or the Old German. The new German that the Germans use today is completely different from the old Plautdietsch used back in the early days when the Bible was first translated from Latin to German. A lot of the verses have a rigid tone because of the German language, which is very precise and to the point. When a person talks about not being conformed to this world, when he says it in German, he says, *"Und Stellet euch nicht dieser welt gleich."* If you translate that the way the German uses the word into English, they can be said either in mild forms or in rigid forms. But if I want to say it in the way the German meant it, I'd have to say, "If the world does it, don't get caught doing it." In English it says, "Be not conformed to this world, but be you transformed." The words are not as rigid in the English as they are in German. I told my Amish neighbor, who is a minister, that if the Amish started using the English Bible, they'd lose the meaning in two generations because they would find themselves in the same boat as that of other churches. Everything in our church is peace and good will and God is love, and that is the way we're trained. But when German words are used, the content comes across a lot differently. There is much more rigidity to it and it is much more demanding in regard to the way we should live and what we need to do to be found in right standing with Him.

Every time I go home and listen to the Amish sermon, all the memories that I knew I could not live with if I wanted to do the things I was gifted to do come back to me. Still, in my older age, a sort of a dilemma is raised for me because it's hard to reconcile the two extremes that I find between the Amish and their thinking and that of the Mennonites. When I go back and listen and see what has happened in the Amish church over all these years and what has happened in the Mennonite Church, there is absolutely no comparison. I would think that if some of those older Mennonite ministers could come back and hear what is being said, they'd probably do somersaults in their graves. I could talk about that for a long time, but there isn't a great deal more I can add to it, other than that the Amish are what they are because of the Martin Luther translation they set for themselves and which all Mennonites live with. All the Mennonites used to use the Martin Luther translation. Of course, the Amish also use Martyr's Mirror a lot in their studies, which is a book I think very few Mennonite people know anything about. Martyr's Mirror is a history of what happened when the Anabaptist life started.

To give you an example of background, my family and my roots go back to the time when Jacob Hochstetler came to this country. He was a dedicated Christian who brought his family to the United Sates and set up housekeeping in Pennsylvania because freedom actually was available to all people in that area. All the Amish who left Europe came because they couldn't find a place where they were actually allowed to stay. The rift came way back in the era when they were just leaving Switzerland and going up into Alsace Lorraine, France. That was when the ministers got together and were talking about some rule changes. What happened was that all of them believed in shunning at the beginning. Jacob Ammon said, "Hey, this is what we believe; we're not going to change." Today, when we read Mennonite history, it is said the Amish left the Mennonites. I would question that because, if you know your facts, you would find that the Amish continued to believe what the Anabaptists believed when they became a religious group.

It just so happens that when you look at what has happened today between the Amish and the Mennonites, you can see a great change. One of the things the Amish were concerned about way back was what should be believed in terms of education. The Amish don't believe in educating anybody beyond the eighth grade. Their idea is that, once something like education is allowed to become uppermost in the minds and hearts of people it's almost an idol. When people make a special effort in not having more than two children so they will be able to best educate them; when they get many degrees themselves just to improve their lots in life; they should, instead, think more back to the time when God took the original man out of the Garden and spoke to him. "By the sweat of your brow shall thou eat thy bread," He cautioned. In German it says, *"Im schweisz deines ungesichts sollst du dein brod essen."* That is something the Amish seek highly, and that's why they have all their private schools. Many of the schools have teachers that have no education beyond the eighth grade, either. What's fascinating is that many times students that go to these schools will end up winning spelling and math contests, showing that when they do go for education, learning how to read and write and spell, they are among the best. First Corinthians, to which they refer, contends that the wise people, educated people, people of the world, will be brought to naught, and the way it's written in German is the reason the Amish think education is not so important beyond just knowing what is required to get through life. They believe in working and of interpreting the word as it's basically written.

Very seldom do Amish vote, and they don't vote because it is stated in the thirteenth chapter of Romans in English that every soul is subject to the higher powers, and that there is no power but the power of God. The powers to be are ordained of God. That is why they believe what they believe. The first chapter of Colossians also talks about that, and it tells in the sixteenth verse that all things were created for Him in Heaven and on Earth, visible and invisible, whether it be thrones, principalities, or powers, all things were created by Him and for Him. That is stated rather strongly. So, because of those statements and the statements in German, which make them stronger yet than what they are stated here in English, they just won't vote. Voting is not something they get involved in. My dad never voted, and I've only voted twice in my life. That's the reason they take the pacifist stand that whatever happens is going to happen. When somebody gets elected, God has a purpose for that. It might be fatalistic in most people's minds, but in the Amish mind, it isn't. They go about their task, which is to do what they think is right and choose not to get involved in the worldly things of government.

An Amish church is usually made up of twenty or more families or homes. Services are held every other Sunday. On the off Sundays, people go visiting in other district churches. Each church, as a rule, has a bishop, two ministers who do preaching, and two elders who look after the people in the church. They step in if a person does err, and another member thinks he or she needs to be visited. They also help raise funds for families who suffer sicknesses or other misfortunes. The elders have tasks different from those of the preachers.

An Amish service is usually three hours, stops before lunch, and then the group gathers together and eats a small meal. When I was a child, that usually consisted of peanut butter bread, some pickles and red beets, and a drink of some kind. I think that has changed somewhat in recent years to be a little bit more of a meal. The services usually start with songs from the German Ausbund, which doesn't have notes of any kind. Usually, a leader starts out with a tune, which is somewhat of a chant, and then the group sings several of the songs. The ministers then retire to the upstairs room to decide what path the service will take that day. Sometimes, a new minister comes to that church, but he will then be the one that makes the main service. Several ministers will take part first. One will have an opening and read a portion of the Scripture and do a prayer, and then the other minister will carry forward some more on it. Then, after that has been carried forth, the bishop will take over and preach the main part of the service. The preacher will then ask the other bishops (they refer to it as Zeugnis), for an evaluation of what the bishop has said and ask whether they agree with it and whether there are any additional thoughts or opinions. If they want to add to it, they can, and if they have some differences of opinion on some technicality, they might make a mild statement about that, but it gives everybody a chance to give honor to the service and to remind everybody of the importance of what was being said.

An Amish wedding is something that is highly prized by all the young girls that want to get married. It is a time when a lot of the boys who have cars will put them away and marry Amish because this is a very important part of life. When I go back and see some of my younger generation coming into the Amish family and watch my sisters' daughters get married, I am reminded of when I was young at home and took part in some weddings, and I see that the process hasn't changed in fifty years. Some Amish wedding customs are quite different from those of other churches. A wedding will last three hours, and several ministers will preside. Much revolves around all the admonition that is in the Bible as to what the man's responsibility is to the woman and what the woman's responsibility is to the man.

The first thing that happens at the service is that the couple getting married is invited upstairs to a special room that has been prepared, where they will be instructed as to how the service is going to take place, and they are reminded of all the commitments they are making. The importance of the vows they are taking is emphasized, and the couple is reminded that they are never to be broken; if they do break them, they will immediately lose their position in the Amish church. The church starts with some singing from the Ausbund, and then the people come downstairs and take their positions; the couple and attendants sit facing each other. Each has a partner sitting on each side of him or her, what they call best man and bridesmaid in other churches. Actually, there is a pair of those; a friend of the man, (or he might have a brother), and a girl is picked to sit opposite him: the bride has a girl friend beside her and a male friend sitting opposite her. Those are the key support people, the cooks and table waiters come into the service about eleven o'clock to see the marriage ceremony. They have quite a number of what are called cooks and table waiters. The service is pretty much like a regular church service but, at about a quarter to twelve, the bishop asks the couple to come up, stand in front of him, and he goes over the vows. They have to respond to him and the pubic. When that is done, a song will be sung, and the service is ended. As a rule, they will then go to another home, where the tables are set up and where everybody is invited to come and join in to eat. After everybody has eaten, they gather around, and they sing out of the Ausbund in German.

Then people go home to their farms, do their chores, and come back in the evening. The couple has invited all of their area friends; if somebody married a person from another district, all the young people from that church are invited, and they try to invite so that there are just about as many young girls as there are boys. And so, in the evening, after the older people have finished eating, the boys will gather around towards the barn, and the girls will stand at the corner of the house where it enters into the area where they are going to sit. The boys will come marching from the barn, one after the other in sequence, and they will select a girl to eat with. The girls will all be standing there with their song books. That is the way they get to learn to know one another, and a lot of them find their mates in life. They sit with each other and visit that evening, eat together, and then start singing songs. Those songs will be from song books that have notes with them, they're not as much a chant and many are in English. That is the way an Amish wedding is conducted.

We have had Amish girls working in our factory. When they get married, they sometimes invite the office workers and other workers in the plant to come to the wedding. There is always some real conversation the next day: How in the world can they ever do that? Why would the girls do it? They just can't believe that the girls stand there, and boys walk up and ask them to go in, and they just don't raise any questions or any objections: they just go with them. That is quite different than it is in some other parts of society.

An exception to this sort of practice is observed by a group of Amish in Berne, Indiana. That settlement of Amish uses the Swiss language and wedding customs that are retained from their homeland. The Berne group of Amish was a small number that stayed in Switzerland and followed the basic beliefs of the Amish, while most of the others left for America. All of the other Amish had scattered throughout Europe before settling in America. Later, the Swiss group also left Switzerland and moved directly to Berne.

I was asked by the Abe Yoder family to take them in my car to an Amish wedding at a home in Berne. I also attended the wedding. I did not understand all of the service because of the use of the Swiss language. When they read out of the Bible, I understood because they used the same Bible as the local Amish do. The ceremony was much like that of the local Amish where I grew up, but things changed after the marriage was completed. The large table spread that was set up for many to sit to eat had a number of punch bowels with homemade red wine in them. Young and old were taking part in drinking wine in toasts to the bride and groom.

That was in the summer time, and the weather was very nice. After dinner, instead of singing out of the German Ausbund, young and old went outside and sat on the lawn in a big semi-circle about ten rows deep, facing the newly married couple. They started to sing and yodel to the couple. They kept that up for a long time. It was the most spectacular demonstration of music by amateur singers I have ever heard. A few Amish played stringed Swiss instruments which added to the presentation.

I will never forget that moment in my life. It was one of the first trips I made with my used 1938 Hudson car.

Now, funerals are quite a bit different. When somebody within the church dies, the body is taken to the funeral home and embalmed, placed into a wooden, homemade casket and brought back to the home for viewing. Usually, no flowers are involved. What amazes me is that all of the people within miles come to pay respect to the family at the viewing– young people, unmarried people, everybody comes. A book or pad is usually placed someplace where visitors sign their names as they come through. Everybody sits, the whole family that is involved or closely related, all the brothers and sisters and close cousins all sit in sequence. Nobody speaks; the visitors just come in and shake each other's hands. Usually, if the husband dies, the wife sits at the head of the row close to the casket. People walk by the casket, which is open viewing, and then they'll shake hands with the wife and all the children and then with brothers and sisters of the deceased and next of kin, who are all sitting there showing their respect. All they do is just acknowledge each other. Very little conversation takes place. This usually happens in the afternoon, starting at two o'clock. At five o'clock, the neighbors come in with a lot of food, and everybody will quit viewing until everybody has eaten. That usually takes an hour. Then they come back in and take their seats again and continue viewing. Hundreds and hundreds of people will come through, which, at times, is just almost unbelievable. Parents, young people with children, the mother with a child in her arms and the father with the older ones, one on each arm, all walk through. They raise the children up and show them the deceased person, and so those children are taught to pay respect to the older people from young up. It's a real experience to be part of that. I have seven sisters, and several of them have lost their husbands now. I have lost both my mother and father and have seen that this same process always happens. It is like it's always been. The funeral service is three hours long because all pass by the open casket again. After the lengthy service, everyone goes out to the graveyard. They usually have six helpers called "pallbearers," who actually dig the whole grave. They put down a rough box and then put the homemade casket in the box. They put wooden boards over it and take turns shoveling the dirt on top. Two of them shovel at a time for ten or fifteen minutes, then two others, then the next two, and then the first ones that started do it again. Sometimes other close relatives help. They mound the dirt up a little bit over the grave so that, as it settles down, it will be even with the ground. During that time, they do some singing, as well as a prayer, while they complete the covering of the body, and then everybody goes back to the house. The neighbor ladies that live in the area have a big meal prepared for all the relatives and friends that want to take part in eating and visiting that afternoon. Many times, people who may have married and moved off into another state come from great distances, so lots of people will get to see friends and relatives they never have a chance to see until such an event brings everybody together. Sadness actually also has some joy mixed with it because people who have not seen each other for years have a chance to get together.

Something else that's different with the Amish is that they don't have paid preachers. They choose their preachers by lot, and everybody in the church who has a chance to vote determines the lot. Any of the men that have over five votes is required to choose a book. No woman has ever been in the lot. It is done by lot principle, just as it was done after Judas betrayed Christ. At that time, a replacement disciple was put in by lot drawing, so that is the method the Amish still use. A new minister is first a minister; later, he can become a bishop. As a rule, elders are not moved up to be ministers, deacons, or bishops.

I failed to elaborate on the importance the Amish place on vows. Deuteronomy, the twenty-third chapter, verse twenty-one through twenty-three says, "When thou shalt vow a vow unto the Lord thy God, thou shalt not slack to pay it: for the Lord thy God will surely require it of thee; and it would be sin in thee. But if thou shalt forbear to vow, it shall be no sin in thee. That which is gone out of thy lips thou shalt keep and perform; even a freewill offering, according as thou hast vowed unto the Lord thy God, which thou hast promised with thy mouth." In Numbers 30:2, 3, and 4 it says, "If a man vow a vow unto the Lord, or swear an oath to bind his soul with a bond; he shall not break his word, he shall do according to all that proceedeth out of his mouth. If a woman also vow a vow unto the Lord, and bind herself by a bond, being in her father's house in her youth; And her father hear her vow, and her bond wherewith she hath bound her soul, and her father shall hold his peace at her: then all her vows shall stand, and every bond wherewith she hath bound her soul shall stand."

The New Testament also has some instructions. In Matthew chapter five, starting at verse 33, it says, "Again, ye have heard that it hath been said by them of old time, Thou shalt not forswear thyself, but shalt perform unto the Lord thine oaths: But I say unto you, Swear not at all; neither by heaven; for it is God's throne: Nor by the earth; for it is his footstool: neither by Jerusalem; for it is the city of the great King. Neither shalt thou swear by thy head, because thou canst not make one hair white or black. But let your communication be, Yea, yea; Nay, nay: for whatsoever is more than these cometh of evil."

That is why the Amish are so solid on marriage vows and not filing lawsuits where witnesses have to get up in front of courts and make oaths. That subject has been talked against through all their lifetimes and is being taught yet today, so very few Amish go to court, and very few of them make an oath or pledge anything.

My ancestral background is quite interesting. We have a Hochstetler book that has recorded a lot of what has happened to the ancestors who arrived from the old country. They were Amish people, and they came and settled in the Pennsylvania area. Jacob Hochstetler was my ancestor's name. He was born in 1712. He was 26 when he arrived in the United States on a ship called the Charming Nancy on November 9, 1738, with his wife Lorentz and his sons John, Jacob, Jr., Joseph, and Christian, and a daughter. They first lived in Brecknock Township in Lancaster County. On May 22, 1751, the family moved to Heidelburg Township in Berks County. That was near Reading, Pennsylvania. Their son, John, married Catherine Hertzler and lived next door to his parents.

The family's relations with the Indians were good until the French and Indian War started. When the French came down from Canada, the only tribe in the area was the Delaware. The government had built many forts along the Susquehanna River, and on north of Harrisburg were other forts. The French stirred up the Indians, telling them they needed to help the French drive the white people out of the area, so a war started between the white settlers and the Indians. That led to several massacres in different areas.

On April 28, 1757, John Adams Miller was scalped near the Hochstetler homestead. One evening in September of 1757, a group of young people was gathering with the Jacob Hochstetler family, slicing and peeling apples for drying. Some of them stayed until late at night to help clean up. When everything was finished, they departed, and the family went to bed. Soon after, the dog started barking. Jacob opened the door to see what was going on. He was immediately shot in the leg by an Indian. More than ten of them were standing out by the bake oven. Jacob's sons, Joseph and Christian, picked up their guns and were ready to defend the family. The father wouldn't allow the boys to shoot at the Indians because he knew that would only start more trouble. The Indians then set fire to the home. The Hochstetler's married son, John, who lived nearby, saw the fire and came to help. When he got there and saw what was happening to his parents, he ran home and hid his own family. Later, he returned to see the bloody mess that had taken place.

Father Jacob had pushed his wife out of the basement window where the couple had gone to seek refuge, and she was immediately scalped and stabbed. Joseph, who was swift and could outrun the Indians, ran and hid himself. Jacob, Jr. and his sister were tomahawked to death. The father Jacob and his son Christian, along with Joseph, then surrendered. Joseph saw his father being captured, and he wanted to stay with him. The Indians burned all the buildings and took the family captive, then went north across the Blue Mountains. The prisoners were forced to dress like Indians and had no knowledge of the fates of one another. They lived for several years in areas as far north and as far west as Erie, Pennsylvania, and some were in the Detroit, Michigan area. Jacob wasn't allowed to keep his beard. It was pulled out of his chin by the Indians' bare hands, and he was forced to wear Indian garments and feathers. As they were separated, the father told his sons never to forget to pray the Lord's Prayer.

Joseph was forced to become a full-fledged Indian because he was a good marksman. He was made to go through many Indian ceremonies to complete his admission to the Indian tribe, but he never felt like an Indian. He was a crack marksman and was forced to go out to gather up game for the rest of the Indians; therefore, he had to travel with them as they moved throughout the countryside.

Jacob also never felt like an Indian. He learned some language in the several years he was with them. Once the Indians were discussing a big river where they might try fishing. Jacob had made friends with John Sprett, a German and also a captive, and they planned to escape together. They traveled in the direction of the big river the Indians had talked about. The first night, they made a fire to cook food, and the Indians stopped by and asked what they were doing. Jacob asked John to go get some sticks to feed the fire. He told the Indians he was going out to look for something to eat. So the Indians stayed nearby, and the German must have found some sticks. When Jacob came back with some food he had acquired, the Indians had left and the fire was burning, but Jacob saw blood standing around the fire, so he decided to flee, and he fled alone. He ran all night and for many days. For several days, he kept traveling in an easterly direction and finally came to a large river. He made a raft of logs and vines and floated it down the river. He hoped he was on the Susquehanna River. However, after many days of travel, he was afraid he might have been on the Ohio River and was going in the wrong direction. He couldn't decide whether or not he was going further and further from his original home. He continued to float down that stream and, all of a sudden, he came to Fort Harris at Harrisburg, Pennsylvania. Jacob had made it back home. People came out from the fort and rescued him after three years of being away from his family. He never knew where he started from or how long it took him to escape because he was so near death when he completed his trip.

Christian returned to his father's home later, dressed as an Indian. His father sat at the table eating and didn't know him. Christian left the kitchen and went out and sat on a stump. After his father finished his meal, he went out to converse with the man he thought was an Indian and, in broken German, Christian said to his dad, "I am Christian Hochstetler." Imagine the joy that brought to his father, who had not seen him for many years. Joseph hadn't seen Christian, either. They had been away from white people for a long time. Christian later found a girlfriend, married, and became a preacher in the church.

In 1762, Jacob prepared a petition to Governor Hamilton from Harrisburg to get all the captured white persons released, according to the agreement that the Indians had made with the state of Pennsylvania when the French and Indian War stopped. That was supposed to be successful in getting Joseph released, but it didn't happen until a couple of years later when Colonel Bouquet was successful in getting him freed. Joseph later married Anna Blank, and they had seven children.

Jacob had remarried to a lady named Anna. Not much is recorded of their family or of where they moved immediately, but they did settle in different places and ended up in Somerset County. I think that is where Jacob was buried. John and some of the others had large families which kept coming further west. Some of them stayed in Somerset County;

Front row (Left to right): Joe Yoder, Ura Gingerich, Anna Graber, Viola Yoder, Ida Hostetler, **Eldon Hostetler**, Violet Mehl, Melvin Graber, Annie Yoder, Freeman Yoder, Ezra Gingerich, and Teacher Mabel Miller. *Back:* Mose Gingerich, Daniel Bontrager, Levi Yoder, Lizzie Graber, Orpha Hostetler, Helen Mehl, Irma Yoder, Will Yoder, Fred Yoder, and Monroe Yoder.

some of the families moved on into Ohio; some went on into Iowa; some of them settled in Elkhart County, Indiana; some of them settled in Marshall County, and some of them in LaGrange County. I had an uncle who lived in Oregon, so it is known that they scattered all over the United States. That is pretty much the history of the way I ended up in Indiana.

I am a descendent of Jacob through his son, John, who had Daniel; Daniel had Jonas; Jonas had David; David J. had David D. Hostetler, and David D. Hostetler was my grandfather. My father was Mahlon Hostetler. That is the way I am tied back to the Hochstetler who came to the United States from Switzerland and was captured by the Indians, which is quite a history. I always get a chill when I travel the toll road and cross the Susquehanna River at Harrisburg, Pennsylvania. I go to Hershey, Pennsylvania for activities during the fall, which always include a big car show. So much for my historical background.

One thing that was interesting to me in school was the attitude of some of the students. Some of them didn't like history, and they'd tell the teacher they didn't much care for it. One time, one of the students in an older class made a comment that he didn't see why we studied old boring stuff that happened hundreds of years ago. Mabel, the teacher said, "It doesn't make any difference. What you do today is already history tomorrow. You'd better learn to appreciate what you do because, if you don't pay any attention to history, you're not going to be very beneficial to society." That really made a big impression on me because I sensed that what she said was very true. I was in about the third grade.

One of the things Mabel had the students do was learn to memorize things. That was something that came pretty easily for me because I could remember things after I heard them. I remember the first story in the first grade reader was *The House that Jack Built*. I still recite that all the way through. There were other poems we had to learn, poems like *Leaves*. It went like this, as I remember it:

> *Scamper little leaves about in the autumn sun,*
>   *I can hear the old wind shout,*
> *Laughing as they run.*
>   *And I haven't any doubt that you like the fun,*
> *But when you have run a month or so,*
>   *Very tired you'll get,*
> *But the same old wind I know will bc laughing yet*
>   *When he tucks you in your snow downy coverlet.*
> *So run on and have your play,*
>   *Romp with all your might*
> *Dance across the autumn sun*
>   *While the sun's still shining bright.*
> *For soon you'll hear the old wind say,*
>   *"Little leaves, good night."*

Another one was:

> *A little robin redbreasl sat upon a tree*
>   *Up went pussycat, down went he.*
> *Down came pussycat,*
>   *Away robin ran,*
> *Said the little robin redbreast,*
>   *"Catch me if you can."*
> *Little robin redbreast sat upon a wall*
>   *Pussycat jumped after him,*
> *Almost had a fall.*
>   *Little robin chirped and sang.*
> *What did pussy say?*
>   *Pussycat said, "Meow,"*
> *Robin flew away.*

Another one was:

How I love to go up in a swing,
Up in the air so blue,
Oh, I do think it's the pleasantest thing
Ever a child could do.
Up in the air and over the wall
Till I can see so wide
Rivers and trees and cattle, and all over the countryside.
Till I look down on the garden green and the roofs so brown,
Up in the air we go flying again,
Up in the air and down.

Another one:

I have a little pussy, her coat is silver gray,
She lives out in the meadow,
Not very far away.
She's always been a pussy,
She's never been a cat.
For she's a pussy willow,
Now what do you think of that?
Meow, meow, scat!

Of course, we all had to try to learn the Gettysburg Address. I can cover it pretty near all, but miss a little bit of it. It gives me great pleasure that I can go as far as I can:

"Fourscore and seven years ago, our fathers brought forth on this continent a new nation, conceived in liberty and dedicated to the proposition that all men are created equal. Now we are engaged in a great Civil War, testing whether that nation or any nation so conceived can long endure. We are met here on the battlefield of that war. We are met here to dedicate a portion of that field as a final resting place for those who gave their lives that this nation might live. It is fitting and proper that we should do this. But in a larger sense, we cannot dedicate, we cannot consecrate, we cannot hallow this ground, but the brave men living and who died here have consecrated it far above our poor powers to add or detract. The world

will little know nor long remember what we say here. But it will never forget what they did here. It is the living rather than the dead to be here consecrated to the great task remaining before us, that we highly resolve that this nation will not have died in vain, but that this nation under God shall have a new birth of freedom, and that the government of the people, by the people and for the people shall not perish from the Earth."

That is not quite correct, but it is the way I remember it.

I had a father who believed in schooling, but he also believed in my being at home as soon as school was out to help work. We only lived a couple hundred feet from the school, and he was going to take over my education from that time on. He had a philosophy that if the teacher suggested I take a book home, I was instructed to leave it in a big culvert that was halfway between the school and my home, leave it there, then pick it up in the morning and take it back to school. I was never allowed to bring a book home until the end of the school year because he was teaching me during those home hours. When I was in school, it was the teacher's job to teach me. So I grew up with that kind of a philosophy, which is considerably different from what is seen today. I never was bothered with back problems because of carrying a backpack!

During the school year, I was almost always called upon to fix anything that needed repair. I lived close to the school and could get tools quickly. How was it possible for me to go to school only eight years, when most everybody else was going eight and a half years? My birthday was December 25, which was almost at the end of that year. Dad never reported my age, and he started me to school the next year, when I would be eight on December 25. The rule then was that pupils didn't need to start at the end of the schooling period if their sixteenth birthdays came before January. Therefore, I wasn't required to take the one half year of grade eight over again. That is what most Amish students were doing at that time.

The most interesting subjects for me in school were geography, history, and arithmetic. English, music, and health were subjects in which I had to put forth some extra effort in order to get a good grade. During the time I went to school, LaGrange County School System had a two-test program at the end of the year. Grades one through six had one test; seven through the last year of high school had the other one. The number of correct answers based on your school gave you a grade score. I remember taking that test in the spring of the eighth grade school year. During that fall, C.F. Kohlmeyer, LaGrange County Superintendent, came to visit with Dad because of my test score. According to him, I had an excellent score, and he thought I should go on to get more education. Dad told him I was going to be an Amish farmer and didn't need more education than what he was going to give me. Mr. Kohlmeyer stated that he was sorry to hear that and started to leave. He then turned and asked Dad where he might be able to get an Amish girl to work during the time his wife was giving birth to a child. Dad had a very short response, stating Mr. Kohlmeyer should get a better-educated girl to do that. His remark ended the conversation.

Even though that removed all thoughts of any further education possibilities on my part, I was sure I was not cut out for farming. When I was seven years old, Grandpa Schrock allowed me to take the Huber tractor and the clover huller to the Joe Yoder farm, located a mile south. I took the unit back into a nearby field and got the clover huller ready and positioned according to wind direction. Grandpa was on another project and couldn't be there at the time. I placed the drive belt on the tractor and on the huller and had everything lined ready for hulling clover when he came. That was always done in the afternoon when it was very dry. As a rule, the first cutting of clover was made for hay, and the second cutting was allowed to grow into maturity for seed. The crop was always harvested with the Birdsell clover huller. That was one of the dirtiest jobs on the farm. Farmers kept doing it because of the value of the seed produced and for the forage from the crops for cattle and horses. That was the first time I was trusted to take such special equipment to the location all by myself.

At fourteen years of age, Dad gave me a team of horses, a wagon, and a pitchfork to help thresh wheat for the neighbors. In the fall of 1936, I was allowed to go help Grandpa with corn shredding. The custom was to cut the corn and put it in a shock at frost time and let it finish ripening. Later in the fall, around the last of October or first of November, it was run through the stationary corn shredder. That unit shredded the stalks and the leaves and separated the ears from the stalks, husked them, and elevated the ears up onto a wagon. The unit had to be hand fed into the snapping rolls. Grandpa and I took turns doing that. The machine was dangerous if the operator didn't keep his hands out of it. When row crop tractors came on the market, many had corn pickers mounted on them. They also were dangerous, and many farmers lost their arms if they didn't keep clear of the units. Cutting corn and putting it in shocks was a practice done by almost all the Amish farmers in the 1940s. In 1942, my last year at home on the farm, my brother David and I cut over a thousand shocks. They were eighty hill shocks of corn. All of that was run through the corn shredder later that year.

As a young boy, one of the most dreaded tasks was taking the young colts and female calves to Grandpa Hostetler's pasture farm land. The pasture was located about five miles from our home. We took the animals loose and chased them all the way. Dad was on the wagon giving instructions on what to do as we approached farm homes so as not to let the animals into their yards. Animals didn't always cooperate. By the time we got there, I was totally exhausted from running to control them. Six months later, we had to bring them back the same way. Today, nobody would ever think of trying something like that. However, in those days we never saw more than one or two cars on the whole trip. When Dad purchased the sixty acres that joined our farm, we discontinued using Grandpa Hostetler's pasture.

Grandpa Schrock decided to stop threshing with so many units. He had listed on his April 20,1937, sale bill the following: one 32-45 Huber Tractor and one 20-40 tractor with the starter that started the way I referred to earlier. He had three threshing machines: a 28-46 Minneapolis Moline, a 32-54 Minneapolis Moline, a 32-52 Red River Special, one Number 8 Birdsell Clover Huller, one 8 roll Dues Steel corn shredder. Later in the year, he purchased a Case Model L tractor to supply a belt power to one of the neighbors who had purchased one of his threshing machines. He found that he couldn't adjust to total retirement.

Chapter 2

My Health Record

My father had a sister, Sarah. She was married to Sam Miller, and they had three boys: Freeman, Milo and Eldon. When I was born, I was named after the last one. Sarah was the oldest child in Dad's family. She had a heart problem that kept her in bed. We went to visit her one Sunday afternoon when I was only three years old. Late in the afternoon, I got into a bottle of strong heart pills that were on her night stand beside her bed. My parents started the five-mile trip home with a horse drawn buggy. After traveling only one mile, I started to vomit and showed signs of severe stomach pains. They passed a home on the way and saw Dr. Eash's car parked in the yard. They stopped and asked Dr. Eash to check me out, which he did. He inserted a tube down my throat and into the stomach to remove the residue. He placed medication into my stomach to counteract the heart pills. I only remember the pain of the tube being inserted down my throat. Memories of the rest of this story are all things I was told in my youth. They were sure I was going to die because of the way I was acting before Dr. Eash worked on me. This story was repeated many times during my lifetime. God must have had other plans for me that made it possible for Dr. Eash to be at the right place at the right time.

During my school years, all of my brothers and sisters and I had the measles, mumps, chicken pox, and whooping cough. Today, children can be vaccinated against all those health problems. Students in my school were hit with the scarlet fever virus. The County Health Department came out and placed a sign with a yellow flag in our yard stating that we were quarantined. It prevented anyone from entering or leaving our home for two weeks. We couldn't send mail, milk our cows, sell milk, gather or sell any eggs. We couldn't touch anything that might transfer the virus to someone else. We had help come in to milk the cows and gather the eggs.

Most all of us children came down with the virus quickly, so we all got over it at one time. The younger ones had more serious effects, but it was like a vacation for the older ones. We had nothing to do. We couldn't send any mail because the mailman wouldn't stop. He left our mail at the neighbors' house. After two weeks, the quarantine flag was removed, and things got back to normal again.

When I was only six years old, Dad purchased a section of tree top limbs that were left after the logs were cut and removed from a wood located about two miles from our home.

With the help of a hired man, he had already cut all the limbs that were usable to correct length, about fourteen to sixteen inches long. In the fall of the year before corn harvest, he decided to split some of the pieces for use in the kitchen stove. I was asked to work between the persons splitting the wood. I was to pick up the split pieces and throw them onto the kitchen wood pile. The bigger wood pieces would be moved onto the living room heater pile. During one of Dad's splitting cycles, I got too close and got cut in the scalp, including the skull. Dad placed me on the buggy with my head hanging overboard so I wouldn't get blood on the buggy and told me to go home to Mother and have it taken care of. When I got home, Mother jumped on the buggy and went for Dr. Eash in Shipshewana to have it sewed together. When Dad came home that evening, she had some words with him that I wasn't privileged to hear. She didn't talk back to him very many other times that I could remember.

One fall evening when I was seventeen years old, I was putting hay into a down chute reservoir, and I started to chill. I went to the house and reported to Mother that I was covered with gooseflesh all over my body. Mother had me place my feet into a foot tub of warm water, and she kept adding hotter water. Dr. Westfall was called; upon his arrival he took my temperature and reported I had the highest temperature he had ever taken. Dr. Westfall had me remove my feet from the hot water tub and gave me a penicillin shot. That lowered my temperature to almost normal in one hour. The hot water in the tub containing my feet was what raised my temperature. Dr. Westfall told us that I had streptococci infection on the kidneys. The high body temperature did hurt my heart rhythm in later years of life. When I started with heart arrhythmia in 1980, all doctors asked if I had rheumatic fever in my youth. I always stated that I didn't.

When I was over forty years of age, my work load began to affect my health. The doctors gave me pills to relax me. Those same pills started to depress me. The combination got me into enough trouble that Edna, my wife, asked my doctor to make an appointment for a complete health check at Mayo Health Clinic in Rochester, Minnesota in the early 1960s. The checkup took a week to complete. I had to answer over one hundred "yes" and "no" questions on a computer card. The questions were only eight basic ones written many different ways. When all tests were completed, we were invited to come into a room for a report on the examination. We found ourselves with two psychiatrists. They first reported on the findings on the function of all the organs in the body. They found some lesions in the stomach referred to as ulcers.

They then started to tell me about my mental test score. Due to the computer test score, they said I was the most rigid person they had ever tested. They also said I was the only person that detected that the questions were few in number but were written differently for a purpose. The doctors wanted to see how my Amish background would affect my responses. I had told them earlier that my father was in total command in our home in my youth. I did not question that situation because I had heard about a father's duties in church.

One psychiatrist believed I was so rigid in my belief because I had inherited that trait from my father, and that I was not accepting things I was involved in as valid. "You have been very successful in your life and feel guilty about it. The guilt is going to depress you further if you don't get a more favorable opinion of yourself."

The second psychiatrist affirmed some of what the first psychiatrist said but added that the Amish faith influenced my depression because I was now involved in a different world than that of my parents. I was involved in the business world, and that could cause mental problems. My children wanted to do things I wasn't allowed to take part in as a child. Trying to cope with all those pressures, as well as the work load was depressing me. They asked me if I had any questions at that point.

I said, "You both had different answers to a question parents might ask if they were to adopt a child about the way the child would develop into an adult. Do the inherited traits have the most effect on the child as stated by the first person or by the second person's statements about the environment the child grows up in?" That question triggered a debate between the two psychiatrists that were there to help me. After several minutes of each defending his thoughts, they stopped and said, "We are here to help you, not to discuss our different thoughts." I told them their discussion helped me more than anything they had said before; they were surprised, and they asked why I said that.

I told them that hearing them discuss how each felt about his thoughts helped me discover that not everything in life can be as rigid as I had made myself believe. I left that room with the belief that I had to lift myself out of my depressed state of thinking on my own. I stopped all medication except the one for the ulcer. I asked God to help me pull out of the negative feelings. I soon went back to work and handled a bigger work load than before. For the rest of my life, I have had to be careful of what I eat because of my stomach. I started to enjoy life and work again. The relationship with the children started to improve, also. When we sat down and discussed our differences, we were able to come to an agreement on most all differences.

Some of the oldest children were old enough to get married and moved on in life. The three younger boys were still in school. Several years later, Dale got married and went into the military service in Germany. Edna and I went to Kaiserlautern to visit him and his wife and we traveled over most of Europe for two weeks.

In 1980, I had a number of experiences when my heart failed to pump blood through my body. I would get light headed because no blood was getting to my brain. Sometimes I couldn't feel my pulse during those failures. Some episodes would last longer than others. When we tried to go to the emergency room, symptoms would be gone before we arrived or before we were taken care of. On several different occasions, a recording unit was strapped onto my body to record arrhythmia problems; none were ever recorded. My doctors suggested that I visit Dr. Swint in Fort Wayne Lutheran Hospital.

I made an appointment and went to see him. A treadmill test showed nothing. However, he placed a patch over my left side at the heart location. He told me how to hold the phone over that patch and dial a particular number when I had a loss-of-heart-pulse feeling again. After several weeks of wearing the patch, I felt it coming on again one morning in the office. I followed Dr. Swint's instructions with the phone with some questions as to how that could possibly work. It did, however; in less than fifteen minutes, the phone rang, and Dr. Swint was on the phone telling me what he saw on the recording machine. He asked me where we purchased our medication. I told him, and he asked me to come back in three weeks after a period of using the medication he was prescribing. He told me the high temperature I had when my feet were in hot water was what caused the arrhythmia problem. I have never had a problem since I started taking a daily pill to control it.

In the start of 2001, I became aware of some trouble when working outside in cold weather. I had shortness of breath, so I went back to Dr. Swint for a complete heart test. That required several trips to the heart clinic. After all of the tests were completed, he said I have a strong heart that showed no problems on the tests. I assured him that I wouldn't accept his findings until he did a heart catheterization. He no longer did those because of his age, but he has a younger doctor at the hospital that does them for him. I went back several days later for that special procedure. When completed, it showed I had 80% blockage at four points, and he couldn't believe that it didn't show on my other tests. I assured him that was why I didn't believe the results of the three previous tests. He asked if I had any questions at that point. I said I had made the many trips to Fort Wayne, Indiana and mentioned it was getting into springtime, and I'd probably be in bed because of heart surgery! I thought he would tell me it would be weeks before he could do the procedure. Then I had a surprise. He asked about Wednesday of the next week, providing no heart replacement surgery interfered. So, on March 21, 2001, I had five bypasses placed in my heart, was in the hospital six days and at home six weeks before returning to work. That covers my health during the years of my life.

Chapter 3

Remarks by My Father

- *When a salesman would stop at our place and try to sell Dad a product that he wasn't interested in, and he had to listen to a high pressure sales pitch, he always made this statement to us: "There's a person you could get real rich on if you would buy him at what he really knows and sell him at what he thinks he knows."*

- *When someone tried to convince Dad of something that he had great doubts about, he would answer with this statement: "A man convinced against his will is of the same opinion still."*

- *When someone told about a success he almost had in something, Dad would answer with this statement: "When you are out in the middle of a lake and your boat starts to sink, don't turn back, but go on. It's no further to the other side."*

- *When someone told him about a great success someone had in a business venture, he would answer with this statement: "That man could fall down into an outhouse pit and come back up wearing a new suit."*

- *When Dad left for town on a rainy day, he gave us tasks to be done before he got back. If asked if we had to do it if it rained, his answer was always the same: "You don't have to if you want to."*

- *When someone told him about losing out on something that he was almost able to accomplish but was too late, his statement always was: "The early bird always gets the worm."*

- *When someone was telling him about the success he had in his efforts in life, Dad's response was: "A quitter never wins and a winner never quits."*

- *Some of Dad's statements applied to farming: "When plowing, don't look back if you expect to plow a straight furrow."*

- *Some farm gate openings left very little space on each side when entering them with some machinery. If one of his sons would remark about how little clearance was left, Dad always answered with the same statement: "It's just as good as if it were a mile on each side so long as you keep the machinery in the middle."*

- *When someone told Dad about how a person had an opportunity on some deal that proved to have been good at the time, his remark was like this: "When you rabbit hunt, if he jumps up at a distance and if you don't shoot, you're surely not going to get him."*

- *When someone told Dad how he was going to do something that would get him rich quickly, his answer was always the same: "Talk's cheap; it takes money to buy whisky." I never saw him buy any, but he used this statement many times.*

- *When someone mentioned time he spent because he failed to do a task quickly enough, his remark was: "A stitch in time saves nine."*

- *When someone told Dad about his debt problems, he had this answer: "When you pay as you go, you never owe."*

- *When Dad asked us to do something quickly, if we questioned why it couldn't wait a little, his remark was always the same: "Wait is what broke the wagon down."*

- *When someone talked about making a profit on low production, Dad had this statement: "Do like the woman that darned socks. She did them for less than the yarn cost: however, she did so many that it made a profit for her."*

- *When someone mentioned to Dad how hard it was for him to decide which product to buy, his standard answer was: "When you enter an orchard, it isn't hard to find where the best apples are: it's where the most big sticks lie under the tree."*

Chapter 4

House Improvements Made in 1950

Soon after moving into our home in the fall of 1949, we started planning what needed to be improved. The need for an inside bathroom became the top priority, but it would have to wait until the spring of 1950. We had to add on to the house for the bathroom area. The water supply was outside in a small building; all water used was carried inside. Kitchen cupboards and a sink were added in the kitchen. We added the width of the bathroom tub to the east of the house. We started the project in the spring, which required adding a septic tank and doing major plumbing to get water pipes to all the locations that needed water. One fine spring Saturday morning, I got busy digging a hole to bury a big metal septic tank. The plumbers had installed the tub, stool, and lavatory in the bathroom. The next step was to get the septic hooked up and get a jet pump installed on the well. I worked all day getting the septic located and hooked to a drain field. I failed to fill the septic tank with water because the well was not hooked up to a jet pump. I left on a trip to the south on Sunday afternoon and called my wife on Monday at noon asking her how the plumbers were doing. She told me she cancelled them because the septic tank was lying on top of the ground. It had rained during the night, and the water had lifted up the tank until it was on top of the ground. That delayed the use of the bathroom for another week. The trouble of digging out the loose ground around the septic hole became twice as large due to cave-ins and water problems. I got the septic tank back into the hole and filled it with water so it couldn't come back up again. The plumbers had installed the jet pump on the well, so it was easy to fill the septic tank.

We next started to remove buildings no longer needed that were in need of repair; the list was quite long. The first one was a combination corn crib with drive under shed that sat between the barn and the house. The roof supports weren't good any more, so we removed it. The next building to go was the woodshed. The roof leaked and needed much repair, so we removed it. The next thing was the small hen house; it also had roof problems, so it was removed. That left us with the barn which had no foundation; it just sat on large stones. But we kept it for several years due to the new addition that was added to it after the barn was moved to that location. In 1976, that combination was taken down along with the home that nobody would want to rent. Then the only building left of the original ones was the corn crib/hog house combination which had started to lean toward the south. We placed supports trying to keep it from going down. We were using it for storage because it had a good roof, but several years later we allowed it to go down and burned it. That removed all of the original buildings that were on that location. The total area has been converted into one big lawn. The only exception is the area used for a small garden. That has a fence around it to keep out rabbits that want to eat our vegetable garden. When all six children were at home, it took lots of food at meal time. We had a large garden out in front for required early things. The soil was sandy and dried quickly when the sun shined. The back garden was bigger and had soil that didn't dry as quickly. We planted corn, tomatoes, popcorn, cucumbers, cabbage, and potatoes and considered those items to be our fall harvest.

Chapter 5

My Trip to New Jersey with Levi Glick

In 1949, my brother-in-law, Levi Glick, came from Oregon to visit. I had plans to go to a Poultry Show to display the E-Z Feeder at the New Jersey State Poultry Convention. I asked Levi if he would join me on that six-day trip. We left early in the morning with the automatic feeder placed on an all steel trailer. I was driving my new 1949 Club Coupe with overdrive. The feeder consisted of these parts: a steel 400 pound capacity feeder hopper drive unit and forty feet of trough with chain and four corners. We went south to US 30, then east through Pittsburgh, Pennsylvania to the Irvin interchange. We traveled the Pennsylvania toll road to the Carlisle exit. That was the extent of the toll road back in 1949. I noticed that people were working in the toll booths when entering and exiting.

We left Pennsylvania for New Jersey for the two-day show. Returning to Carlisle, Pennsylvania to the toll road when heading toward home, we saw a GI standing at the entrance looking for a ride. We picked him up and proceeded to the toll booth. When I received the toll ticket, it was different. They had gone to a new system. It was night time driving, but the traffic was light, so I put the "peddle to the metal," and we arrived in Irvin, Pennsylvania in record time. I noticed that a Pennsylvania trooper was parked beside the toll booth. The toll booth operator put my ticket in his new machine and asked me if I had the trailer when I entered the toll road. I told him I had. He opened the other side of his booth and said to the turnpike officer, "I didn't think this thing would always work. This ticket tells me this man drove almost 90 miles an hour all the way from Carlisle, Pennsylvania pulling a trailer, ha, ha." I paid and left. The GI hitch hiker who was in the back seat and had not said a word during the whole trip made this remark, "It's no wonder they wouldn't believe it, nobody would, only the one sitting in the back seat scared to within an inch of his life would." We left the G.I. off in downtown Pittsburgh, Pennsylvania for his home on US 30.

On the west side of Pittsburgh, Pennsylvania, I asked Levi if he would consider driving. We stopped, and he got behind the wheel while I got in the back seat to try and get some sleep. Levi had slept during my driving period. I soon dozed off. After some time, Levi failed to turn at an intersection and got off US 30 onto a secondary road. He came to a high railroad crossing, and he failed to slow down enough for it. I flew up against the roof of the car and got wedged — between the seats! — upside down. By that time, I was wide awake and thought the car was also upside down. I yelled for Levi to turn off the switch. He assured me we were right side up, but I was still wedged between the seats upside down. He stopped and helped get me right side up. We turned around and found US 30 again. He never forgot that trip. Whenever Levi would come for a visit, the first thing he would say was, "turn off the switch."

Chapter 6

The History of the Pashan School

The Pashan School was located in the northwest corner of Section 21 in Newbury Township. Present day location would be US Highway 20 and County Road 1000W on the southeast corner (a brick home is located there now). Section 21 was 320 acres, and it was owned by Nelson Rockwell in 1840, which was the year that the school and store were built. In 1846, Joseph Miller paid Nelson Rockwell $1,000 to purchase 160 acres of Section 21. That area was where the school and store were located. The school was small and was located on one-fourth acre of land. It had four walls, windows, and a front door but with no cloak rooms or water pump. It was a fun place for gatherings, spelling bees, singings, writing lessons; it was also used by tramps, hitchhikers, and gypsies. The land was next sold to Jacob P. Schrock who owned it until 1865. Jacob then sold it and the Pashan store for $9,500 to John Johns. Johns sold it to his son, Jake, in 1892. Jake then donated an acre of land to enlarge the school. Levi Eash was a teacher in the small school for one year. Malinda Mehl was the teacher during the last year in the small school and the first year in the new. On a separate sheet at the end of this section, I have a list of all the teachers that taught school at Pashan from 1921 until the year it was closed in 1967.

The new school was built to LaGrange County specifications: wood platform out in front, recessed center door entrance, rope hanging inside on the wall to ring the overhead bell for study period signals. To the right, was the girls' cloak room and to the left was the boys' cloak room. It was understood that the boys had to stay out of the girls' cloak room. The school had many windows and two round wood burning stoves located to provide even heat. The study seats were double wide, and some classes had to use two people per seat. If the class had more than six pupils, the seats were fastened together in units of four and fastened to a wood strip on each end. The school was wide enough to have eight rows of seats, one for each year of school. A blackboard covered the whole width of the school. Library shelves for books that the County changed at times were on the north wall. On the outside was an open hand pump that had a cover built after 1940. There were two outhouses located in the back of the school; the boys' and girls' were on the same side as the cloak rooms. You had to have permission from the teacher to use them. After Jake Johns had the new school completed, he sold the Pashan location to Joas Yoder, who then sold it to Mose Miller, who sold it to Samuel E. Weaver. He lived there only two years and sold it to Fred Suntheimer who sold it to David Schrock, in 1920. David Schrock's daughter, Lizzie, married my father, Mahlon Hostetler, in 1922. They purchased 80 acres on half of the 160 acres that was a part of the many above transactions.

I started school in 1930. Reverend D.D. Miller's daughter, Mabel Miller, taught me the first five years, and there were six students in my class. I know that one-room school house teaching was a big help to me. It was easy to get good grades because I could remember what was said when classes were held in the higher grades, so I already knew the answers. My first year teacher also made us memorize many things. When I started school, my father told me, "When you go to school with your books, they are to stay there; that's why you go to school — to learn what they want to teach you. If the teacher wants you to take a book home to study, I want you to do this: You know the big culvert across the road between home and the school, place your books there on the way home and pick them up the next morning. The only time I want the books home is at the end of the school year. When you are in school, you learn what they want you to learn; when you are home, I'll teach you what I want you to learn." I was the oldest, but everyone younger got the same message.

When Mabel was the teacher, we had a chance to play one game of softball a year with another school. To be able to buy balls and bats, we needed money. We had a plan that we would gather bittersweet at a fence row of the Joe Yoder farm in the fall. The bittersweet would open up and look nice for several months. We made it into wreaths and bunches and took turns standing out along US Highway 20 selling wreaths for fifty cents and bunches for fifteen or twenty-five cents, depending on the size.

At the conclusion of Mabel's career, she had a treasure hunt to disclose her wedding plans. Whenever anything needed to be fixed, she called upon me because we lived close by and had tools to fix things. She asked me the last day of school to fix something, so I went home to get tools for it. Mother said, "Look at this, Mabel is getting married to William Jennings." I went back to school and told Mabel that I knew what the treasure hunt was all about. Mabel asked me if I could keep it a secret, and she promised me something. Mabel also said, "If someone discloses the secret, I'll know you didn't keep your promise." Mabel left this poem about her plans to marry at the last location. It read like this:

On May the 12th I'll wedded be
To William Jennings of Tennessee
My future home will be in that State
So come and visit either soon or late.

It was hard to keep my mouth shut during the hunt. We had to go to many different locations before we found the poem.

Each Monday morning, she would call on someone, most often sixth and eighth grade pupils, to recite a Bible verse. After the Bible verse was repeated, we all took part in this Morning Prayer:

> *Father, we thank thee for the night*
> *and for this new morning light*
> *for rest and food and morning care*
> *and all that makes this world so fair*
> *help us to do in all work or play*
> *to grow more loving in all we say.*

She had a very pleasant way of keeping things under control; if that didn't work she would take a student to the cloak room. When Mabel left teaching, Olive Weaver taught me sixth and seventh grade. Olive was married during the second year to Mel Bontrager. During the last year of school, Pashan had Carrie Yoder for a teacher.

Payson Hostetler is the oldest living person that could give me information on teachers and the years of school at Pashan.

I enjoyed school and tried to learn all I could in the years I had there. We had to take part in Christmas programs that required memorizing parts. In my first school year reader was the short story, "The House that Jack Built." I can still repeat all of it and the poems about nature, songs, and anything that concerned our Christmas programs. During my first year of school, we had a presentation done by a boy and a girl at the Christmas program that went like this:

> *I'm the welcome boy, you see, and I'm the welcome girl, you see,*
> *It gives us both the most delight to see this great big crowd tonight.*
> *It makes us feel that we must do the very best we can for you,*
> *So, all along the smiling way, we'll bow our best this Christmas day.*
> *We bow as low as we can go and end up again like a toy,*
> *I'm the welcome girl, you see, and I'm the welcome boy.*

As a family, we still sing one of the Christmas songs that was sung as an opening in our Christmas program during my second year in school.

My mother, Lizzie, also went eight years to Pashan School, but I have no record of her teacher. Her mother, Anna Bontrager, went to Pashan School for three years. I'm the oldest of thirteen children, four deceased, and we all attended Pashan School. My youngest brother, LaVern, thirty years younger than I am, was in the seventh grade when all one-room schools were closed in LaGrange County in 1967. LaVern then went to Westview School for the last part of his schooling.

Dad purchased the school building from the County and removed it. The County then sold the one and one-fourth acres of land, which he also purchased. When he received the abstract on the land, he found that if the school should be discontinued, the building and the land would revert back to the adjoining farm. Dad went to his attorney and asked about that. He was asked what he had paid for it, and Dad told him how much. The attorney's response was, "I can get all of your money back, but it will cost you more than what you paid for it."

Pashan School Teachers were:

1921-1922 .... Bessie Miller	1945-1946 .... Benjamin Teple
1922-1923 .... Bessie Miller	1946-1947 .... Miss Anderson
1923-1924 .... Bessie Miller	1947-1948 .... Darvon Meyers
1924-1925 .... Walter Babb	1948-1949 .... Benjamin Teple
1925-1926 .... Irene Troyer	1949-1950 .... Amos Hostetler
1926-1927 .... Irene Troyer	1950-1951 .... Amos Hostetler
1927-1928 .... Irene Troyer	1951-1952 .... Amos Hostetler
1928-1929 .... Mabel Ann Miller	1952-1953 .... Amos Hostetler
1929-1930 .... Mabel Ann Miller	1953-1954 .... Amos Hostetler
1930-1931 .... Mabel Ann Miller	1954-1955 .... Amos Hostetler
1931-1932 .... Mabel Ann Miller	1955-1956 .... Amos Hostetler
1932-1933 .... Mabel Ann Miller	1956-1957 .... Amos Hostetler
1933-1934 .... Mabel Ann Miller	1957-1958 .... Duane Schrock
1934-1935 .... Mabel Ann Miller	1958-1959 .... Duane Schrock
1935-1936 .... Olive Weaver	1959-1960 .... Irene Gage
1936-1937 .... Olive Bontrager	1960-1961 .... Irene Gage
1937-1938 .... Carrie Yoder	1961-1962 .... Irene Gage
1938-1939 .... Carrie Yoder	1962-1963 .... Irene Gage
1939-1940 .... Helen Mishler	1963-1964 .... Irene Gage
1940-1941 .... Olive Bontrager	1964-1965 .... Irene Gage
1941-1942 .... Helen Mishler	1965-1966 .... Irene Gage
1942-1943 .... Dorsa Mishler	1966-1967 .... Irene Gage
1943-1944 .... Katherine Miller	1967-1968 .... Westview
1944-1945 .... Katherine Miller	

Chapter 7

What Led Me to My Life's Vocation

My father's older brother's daughter, Katie Hostetler, was being married to Perry Glick, and I was invited to the wedding. At that time, Amish boys who owned cars weren't always appreciated at social gatherings. Only three boys who owned cars and were not Amish were on farms in northern Indiana at that time. In most homes where a son had a car, he was required to leave home and was forced to find non-Amish friends.

I was draft-deferred on my dad's farm. At Katie's November 30, 1941, wedding, I was introduced to Mary Glick, a cousin of the groom. The Amish have a wedding custom of having married persons eat first at evening meals. After they have eaten, the young boys and girls of dating age — 16 to 26 — pair up to eat. After an introduction, I asked Mary if she would consider joining me, and she accepted. After the couples had finished eating, the custom was to remove the plates to make room for song books. The young people then sang for the newly married for about an hour. I asked Mary at the dinner whether she would consider a date some week-end. Her answer was, "I have to think about it." Sometime later, I received a letter stating that she would be in Topeka (a near-by town) on Saturday evening, where we could meet. I wasn't sure that was a good way to start a date. I knew she expected me to take her home.

Some Amish parents weren't friendly when daughters came home in a car owned by her date. I knew about that because I was sometimes asked to drive Amish boys to Nappanee, Indiana to date Amish girls. The girls would be in town to be picked up, and they would be delivered home in my car later in the evening. Sometimes, one of the parents came to see whether the girl was with an Amish boy or whether she spent time with a boy that owned a car. Many Amish parents kept close check on what their children were doing.

I went to Topeka to see whether Mary Glick was there on Saturday evening. She was there with a few other girls. We met and went with one of the other girls to visit a home where the parents were on vacation. I was sure Mary expected me to take her home, and I did. I parked out by the road, and Mary invited me into her home where lights were still on. Her mother was finishing her ironing, but she stopped to visit with me. That was the start of a relationship that didn't grow very strong because the father didn't seem friendly.

Soon after that relationship started, a girl named Edna Yoder came to the Glick home one Sunday afternoon with Levi Glick's family. He was Mary's older brother who was married to Irene Yoder, a sister of Edna Yoder. Soon after I arrived, I asked Mary whether she and Edna would like to go meet my sisters. They agreed, so I took Mary and Edna back to my home for several hours. Edna's parents had been Amish until a few years earlier when they left and joined a church that allowed cars and telephones, Levi's family also joined it. My father was impressed with Edna's personality. I was, also, and that was why I had asked them to my home. Edna's parents lived south of Nappanee, Indiana which was about forty-five miles from my home. The time was during World War II when gas and tires were hard to get. I lived on a farm and had the only car on it, so I was able to get more tires and gas than other people could. The Amish boys that hired me to go to see girlfriends in Nappanee gave me R-stamps for gas and paid mileage for the trips. Mary had told me she was joining the Amish church, and that gave me a reason to stop seeing her.

It was then possible for me to check with Edna on the possibility of dating when I was in her area. Dating her, the car wasn't a problem. We started to see each other when I had Amish boys to take along to pay for the gas. My weekly allowance wasn't much, so all I had was what I got from hauling Amish at night and during slow or rainy periods.

Edna's brother, Joe, was employed at Creighton Brothers in Warsaw, Indiana, the largest leghorn farm and hatchery in the United States. He was just older than Edna. When Japan bombed Pearl Harbor, Joe and many other Nappanee boys signed up for armed service. When Joe was ready to leave, he advised me to check out Creighton Brothers for work. Dad had me deferred on his farm operation, but he knew I wasn't interested in the Amish type of farming. My younger brother David had a greater interest in horses and farming than I had. Therefore, Dad told me that when David was eighteen years old, I would need to look for other employment. On January 2, 1944, I went to Creighton Brothers to check for work. I arrived about 10:00 A.M. for the interview. The first question asked me was about where I came from. I told them I was from LaGrange County near Shipshewana, Indiana. They wanted to know how I found out about them. I told them I was dating Joe Yoder's sister, and that he worked for Creighton Brothers until he left when Pearl Harbor was bombed. The next question was whether I also planned to enlist. I told them I was deferred on a farm by a draft board in LaGrange County; it would be left to them to decide where I was needed.

Hobart Creighton was speaker of the Indiana House of Representatives at that point. Hobart's brother, Russell, was in charge of cattle. They farmed several thousand acres of land. They had many hogs and cattle and raised replacement pullets on range. John Frederich was manager of poultry operations and asked me the most questions. I told John that if they wanted to get a deferment for me on their operation, I would let the draft board know where I was. He told me to do that and asked when I was prepared

Creighton Brothers' main office, shell egg processing, feed mill complex, and shop, located 3½ miles west of Warsaw, Indiana on Old Road 30.   *Photo from Creighton Brothers 50th Anniversary promotional flyer printed in 1975.*

to start working. I said, "Any time," and he said to go get some lunch and come back in the afternoon. I was required to work seven days a week on alternative weeks to relieve the workers in the laying houses so they could attend church. My first week's work was catching leghorn pullets on range and moving them into laying houses for egg production. That was in January of 1944, it was cold outside, and I had no warm clothes. However, I couldn't catch pullets wearing gloves! On Saturday afternoon, I received permission to go home for my warmer clothes.

I told my dad about my new job and what the pay was going to be. I had to work ten hours a day which was what I was doing at home. Pay was six dollars a day, and I had to work every other Sunday. Dad's response was to wonder how in the world they could expect to stay in business paying workers that much on a farm operation. When he needed additional help, he paid two dollars a day for farm work.

In several weeks, after the pullets were all housed, I was transferred to night work in the hatchery after another employee left. My job was traying eggs that went into the many Petersime incubators they had running. Eggs were set on Sunday and Wednesday so they would be ready to come out of the incubators twenty-one days later for delivery. Cardboard chick boxes had to be made to ship those chicks. After each hatch on Sunday and Wednesday, the hatcher compartments had to be thoroughly cleaned for the next hatch. That was to keep naval infection from becoming a problem on a hatch of new chicks. At midnight, chicks were taken out of the hatcher to be sexed by the chicken sexor. He separated the pullet chicks from the males. He could do about one thousand an hour. They had to be boxed about two hours before he could do them accurately. The chicks that went west had to be counted and labeled to their destination and taken to the railway express station in Warsaw before five o'clock for the Monday and Thursday morning trains that stopped for the special delivery panel truck. The chicks that went east were done by the daytime workers later in the day. The hatching period stopped at the end of May.

When the hatching season was over, I was moved to the egg grading plant to help pack eggs according to size. All eggs traveled over a light and were inspected for cracks, blood spots, and other forms of rejection.

When fall school time started, John asked if I would consider taking a short course taught by the State Poultry Association at Purdue University. Creighton Brothers Hatchery was a certified hatchery, and that required all birds to be selected and blood tested by someone who had taken the course. It was a hands-on handling of live birds. All birds had to be tested, and those infected with pullorm had to be removed; birds with other defects also had to be identified. I was able to complete both parts of the two-part test — the selection of birds and the blood testing part. That was the first year at Creighton Brothers. Because of my Purdue certificate, I was in charge of blood testing every leghorn pullet that was housed when the fall bird housing started. I did that in the fall of 1944 and 1945. After testing and housing were completed in 1946, I moved to Goshen, Indiana.

A photo of the employees of Creighton Brothers taken during the summer of 1944. I am in the third row, second from right.

Chapter 8

Why Construct A Square 110' Poultry House?

We had made a trip to New Jersey in 1948 to check out the merits of a 150 foot diameter round poultry house construction. We found that the pie shaped rafters required extra lumber to support the roof design. A square building design would be much cheaper to build.

During my travels installing automatic feeders in the south, I came across a large privately owned and operated saw mill. They sawed only White Pine lumber in all thicknesses and lengths. It was far better quality than what was available in Indiana. They also had kiln dried lumber available.

I stopped at the mill and left plans on a 110 foot square poultry building I had planned to build in the fall. Why a square poultry house? That is the cheapest way to get square footage covered, four times 110' is 440' of wall space and have 12,100' of floor space covered. When you build a 40' X 300' poultry house, you have 680' of wall space or

An aerial view of my square chicken house, built in the fall of 1950.

foundation and 12,000' of floor space. To check the birds, you have to walk 300 feet to the back end, and back up to the entrance is 680 feet. In the 110' building, much less distance is involved in checking all the birds.

They sent me costs on the White Pine lumber required for the roof on the 110' square poultry house. The walls were going to be cinder blocks. I couldn't believe how much less they were on lumber costs F.O.B. in the state of Arkansas. The next question was how much it would cost to get it delivered because they didn't deliver to this area. I contacted a trucking company north of LaGrange to see if they would be interested in hauling the lumber back to my location. They checked with the mill on weight and bulk. They came up with a cost for delivery. That lowered my poultry house costs considerably. The lumber had far less knots in it than what was available at local lumber yards. We built the square poultry house in the fall of 1950.

The trucking company started to haul lumber for many builders that were building new poultry houses in LaGrange County. They later established a lumber supply location near State Road 9 and the toll road location in order to supply builder needs.

I used my poultry house for testing many types of new feeding and watering poultry equipment. I didn't cement the floor when the house was built. Several years later, during the years when cement was hard to get, I was asked by a lumber yard in LaGrange whether I would consider taking a rail carload of extra cement they had on hand due to an order mix up. They gave me a price that was hard to refuse, so they delivered the cement to my poultry house. To get someone to mix that much cement by hand was not easy. The entrance door was 8' high, so only a low level gravel truck could enter the building. We found just one truck in the county that was low enough to enter. We mixed all the cement that it took to cover the 12,100' of floor space by hand. It was so much nicer to clean and keep the floor level with litter. When I started to store antique cars in 1983, it was great that the floor was already cemented. We double insulated it and added controlled heat and air conditioning, along with humidity control.

I had added an egg processing room in 1955 to process and hold hatching eggs. That was done because of the upcoming work on my cross-breeding program.

At the present time, that room is being used to house all my Hudson display cases that are full of memorabilia and Hudson parts.

Chapter 9

Why I Don't Vote as a Mennonite Church Member

I was born into an Amish family and went to that church the first eighteen years of my life. I got a car and a driver's license when I was 18 years old. I also got permission to join the Conservative Mennonite Church. I have found that the teachings received in a child's early years are very influential. I'm now eighty-four years old and can speak to that belief. My father never voted when I was at home, and the church spoke and taught that God ordains all governments. Members were told that God might have a purpose for certain rulers to be elected, that people who vote are part of the world system, and that we aren't supposed to be part of it. That is what I heard during my youth attending the Amish church. After I joined the Conservative Mennonite Church, things changed. When Eisenhower ran for president, most Mennonites didn't want a military man to be elected, so I voted against him. I learned later that was my mistake. God had other plans. When Kennedy entered the presidential race, again many Mennonites thought he was a Catholic and that would influence his decisions in government. So I voted against him, also, but he was elected president. Those events have given me assurance that what I heard as a young man is true, that God is in control of elections if we only trust him. God's word has many references to this teaching. When Joseph was sold to Egypt, God used him for a purpose. God also used the king Nebuchadnezzar to punish Israel for its failures in obeying God. We are instructed to pray for our leaders that God has ordained.

In 1966, my wife and I joined the North Goshen Mennonite Church.

Today, God will deal in his own way with the hatred that is continually expressed by certain persons at the elected president. The New Testament has things to say about our conduct toward government.

Romans 13:1-3

13:1 Let every soul be subject unto the higher powers. For there is no power but of God: the powers that be are ordained of God.

13:2 Whosoever, therefore, resisteth the power resisteth the ordnance of God: and they that resist shall receive to themselves damnation.

13:3 For rulers are not a terror to good works, but to the evil. Wilt thou then not be afraid of the power? Do that which is good and thou shalt have praise of the same.

Colossians 1:15-17

1:15 Who is the image of the invisible God, the first born of every creature.

1:16 For by Him were all things created, that are in heaven, and that are in earth, visible and invisible, whether they be thrones, or dominions or principalities, or powers: all things were created by Him and for Him.

1:17 And he is before all things and by him all things consist.

1 Peter 2:13-15

2:13 Submit yourselves to every ordinance of man for the Lord's sake: Whether it be to the king as supreme:

2:14 Or unto governors, as unto them that are sent by him for the punishment of evildoers, and for the praise of them that do well.

2:15 For so is the will of God, that with well doing ye put to silence the ignorance of foolish men:

These are the scriptures that the Amish preachers used to tell their members that it wasn't necessary to vote, that God will take care of them to fulfill his purpose in the world order. I only voted twice and found myself appointed to jury duty each time in the state of Indiana. I think that was God's way of sending me a message. I stopped voting and was blessed beyond measure. I try to daily pray for our elected leaders, whoever they might be that God happened to place there. I find it more troublesome to pray for some than others, but that is my problem, not Jesus' who will judge all men in the end time.

John 5:22-23

5:22 For the Father judges no man, but hath committed all judgment onto the son:

5:23 That all men should honour the Son, even as they honour the Father. He that honoureth not the Son honoureth not the Father which hath sent Him.

I hope this information sheds some light on the way and the reason the Amish deal with the subject of voting. In Indiana, they are also kept off jury duty by not voting.

Chapter 10

Development of the White Meateor Bird

During my employment at Creighton Brothers in Warsaw, Indiana I became manager of the hatchery and had to take my turn working in laying houses on Sundays. Creighton Brothers was involved in producing eggs and replacement baby chicks that would live and become high egg production hens. That was done by bird selection and trap nesting. Trap nesting was a program in which some hens were leg banded with numbers. The nest holes were equipped with wire trap doors and, when the hens entered the nest, they were locked in until eggs were gathered. The individual who gathered the eggs had to write the leg band number of the hen on the egg. Those eggs were placed in the incubators, grouped together, and records were kept on the number of eggs laid by each hen per month. Eggs were grouped together on incubating trays from egg numbers. When placed in hatchers at eighteen days, they were put in separate wire baskets to check for hatchability. All baby chicks hatched from that program were wing-banded and called Record of Performance baby chicks.

That hands-on work gave me added opportunity to learn about poultry genetics. The State Poultry Association was located with Purdue University. That group required that all R.O.P. chicks that were sold had to be blood tested and selected by a state approved licensee. After the hatching season ended at the end of May, Creighton Brothers sent me to the Purdue University Poultry State Association to take a three-week short course. The school was set up to train people to learn how to identify some of the blood transmitted diseases. That was done by placing a drop of blue antigen on a porcelain plate. The next step was to mix one drop of the hen's blood with the antigen and allow one minute of time to see whether a reaction occurred. If there was a reaction, the hen was a carrier of the Pullorum disease, and it was removed. Over seventy people were in the class, and we all had to handle live birds. I passed the test of testing and selecting birds for State Association approval. I was then given the task of blood testing the 500,000 pullets that were housed that fall; I did that for the three years I was employed at Creighton Brothers.

During that period, I saw what could be done with poultry through selection and testing. It was hands-on work, and I was able to see the results when it was done correctly. I was aware that many broilers were being grown in northern Indiana for the live markets in Chicago, Detroit, and Cleveland. That market required a much larger hatchery operation to supply the needs of the broiler growers; birds were replaced every seven weeks. The egg hatching season for layers was mostly a six-month season in the 1940s. I was approached by Doc Pringle, a veterinarian in the Goshen, Indiana area who was interested in starting a hatchery for broilers.

When I moved from Creighton Brothers to Pringle Poultry Farm, I told him about my hobby and said I would move to his place only if I could continue it. He consented, and I moved to the Goshen area to start a new hatchery for broiler chick production. We put up a small building and bought two small Robbins incubators for it. We were never able to supply chicks for large broiler houses. We didn't have the eggs or capacity for it. After several years, Cleo Lambright asked me if I would help him start a bigger hatchery. I also told him about my two goals in life: to develop a new cross breed and to make an automatic feeder. He agreed with mild reluctance, but I started making plans to move to the LaGrange, Indiana area to help build his hatchery.

In the fall of 1948, we moved to one of his farm houses located south of the hatchery location on US Highway 20. I helped complete the hatchery and told him that I was going to work more on my hobby projects. He did not approve of that. One day he told me that we were going to Purdue to meet with State Poultry Association personnel. We went the next day, and I found myself being told that I should quit trying to do things that I wasn't qualified to work on. That suggestion was made into an order that I must observe. I resigned my position as hatchery manager, and we moved to my present location and continued work on both projects.

I had already started a program as a hobby trying to cross-breed a better white bird for the processing plants. It was started in 1945, using four different breeds of birds: Garrison White Cornish, Holsopple White Rock, New Hampshire Reds, and Columbian Wyandottes. Those were picked for specific reasons: the White Cornish for the breast meat, the White Rock for fast feathering, the New Hampshire for fast growth, and the

The new breed of chicken, White Meateor, I developed. The breed was named by contest during the 1949 Elkhart 4-H Fair in Goshen, Indiana.

Columbian Wyandotte for the large body. Using those four different breeds, I was hoping to capture those four traits into one bird, also to end up with a totally white bird having good breast meat, fast feathering, fewer pin feathers, faster growth—an overall bigger bird with better feed conversion. The southern states were starting to use all white birds in broiler production. Northern Indiana growers were all using Barred Rock. When processed, the New Hampshire cross had many black pin feathers. The number one birds from the Cornish White Rock hatch came off looking good. They developed into nice white birds. The number two cross between the New Hampshire Red hens crossed onto the Columbian Wyandotte male resulted in birds of many shades of color and sizes. By saving the eggs and hatching more settings every two weeks, I got a good number of birds to select.

I couldn't find a good used small incubator for sale, so I made one with old and used electric brooder stove parts. It was made with two compartments: the eighteen-day incubating compartment and the three day hatching compartment. It was quite small but produced good hatching performances. When fully loaded, it incubated only several hundred eggs at a time.

I had some used Brower chick batteries that we used to start the new hatched birds. At ten days of age, they were placed on the floor. Several generations of birds per year could

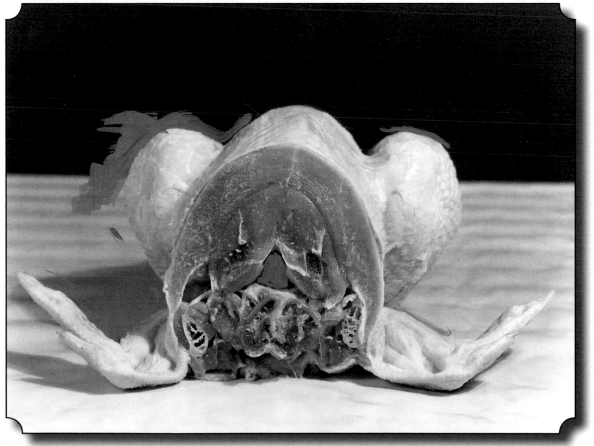

A photo used for advertising the White Meateor shows off some of the benefits of the new breed of chicken.

result from doing that. When males mated with a hen successfully, they fertilized a total of seven eggs that could be laid over a ten-day period and hatched. Sometimes a problem developed when ten hens were placed in a pen with one male in a controlled program. At times, some hens chose not to mate with the one and only male. That stopped the test program because the eggs were not hatching. That was a lot of work, but I could see things improving in the number two cross program. I kept getting more white birds than I could use. The number one cross had only one problem. The males, because of their size, had some problem mating with the hens; fertility on some eggs wouldn't hatch.

There was no established name for the new breed of chickens. In 1949, during the Elkhart County 4-H fair, we rented a space to display some dressed birds and also some live ones. A contest was had for people to view them and then suggest names for them.

An offer of one hundred dollars was made for the winning suggestion. That was paid to a citizen from the Wakarusa, Indiana area who suggested White Meateor. We had an artist take a drawing of a meteor and place the White Meateor name on it as a registered trade mark. After that, all chicks sold were called White Meateor chicks. After twelve generations of inbred crosses were completed, we had an all white bird in number one and number two crosses.

It was then time to try for the new male birds. That was accomplished by crossing the

The logo developed for the White Meateor breed.

number one cross male onto the number two cross female. Guess what happened? I had birds of every color and size again — some totally black, some as small as bantam's birds. The hens were then leg banded and placed in small pens, ten hens per pen and one male. We set up four pens like that in order to find the genes that were causing the problem. The hens were trap nested, and the eggs were marked to hens and hatched separately. Only a few were found that were off color. We got rid of all the others that were causing the off color, and things improved rapidly after that. The inbreeding program continued until all birds were white.

During that period, we had a flock of White American breeder hens for the Farm Bureau Co-op hatchery which supplied broiler chicks to the local trade. I asked if I could use ten of their birds to try crossing the male of my inbred line on those ten White American hens, and they allowed me to do it. The result from that cross was way beyond expectations! The White American breed for broilers was brought to the United States from Holland by the Farm Bureau Co-op hatchery for their broiler growing program. The breed was developed by crossing a Dutch Barnvelder male on a White Leghorn female hen. The offspring for laying dark brown eggs were selected during several generations. The hens had large type combs and white ear lobes, and the hens had much larger bodies than normal White

Leghorns. The White American hens crossed with the White Meateor male grew very fast in my Brower batteries. At three weeks of age, they were marketed as Cornish hens. When Farm Bureau removed the breeder hen flock, we got ready for White American broiler chicks. We kept the best four thousand pullets for breeder hens to produce hatching eggs. Those were crossed with White Meateor males.

I had no hatchery myself to hatch the eggs when my breeder hens started to lay. Contact was made with Nellan's Poultry Farm; they had shut down their hatchery during the time I worked at Creighton Brothers. When called, Max Nellan must have been in a good mood because he agreed to custom hatch our eggs on a fixed cost per case of eggs. We started to deliver close to eight cases of eggs per week. They hatched well; that gave us close to 15,000 chicks per week in sales. I had purchased an International walk-in panel truck for the eighty mile round trip of delivering eggs and picking up chicks. The broiler growers were soon asking for more chicks than we could supply because of the size of our breeder hen flock. The Nellan's Poultry Farm had empty hen houses.

Above: Nellan's Poultry Farm.

Left: The walk-in panel truck I purchased for delivering eggs and picking up chicks.

Max was asked if he would consider putting in breeder hens because of the demand for more chicks. He agreed to start White American chicks and keep the pullets for cross breeding with White Meateor males. That more than doubled our egg supply. We started to cut into the Lambright Hatchery's broiler chick customers. I had helped him to start his hatchery, but was now cutting into his market with a cross bred bird that he thought wasn't going to amount to anything. I left his operation because I was not able to continue in the development of the automatic feeder and the cross bred chicken.

More trips were required to Mentone, Indiana due to increased demand for chicks and eggs for the hatchery. It was becoming a much bigger project than I ever expected. Requests for more chicks in outlying areas started to develop in Michigan and Ohio. I had made a winch cable suspended watering trough for the breeder hens. It was done to see whether birds would spill water out of it. The test line proved that hens preferred this because the floor under it was drier. People who saw it were asking how soon they could buy it. That caused additional pressure on me to make a decision on what to do with the White Meateor chick sales demands that were getting way beyond our ability to supply. The Nellans had a lot more work than expected with the addition of the breeding flock and additional hatchery work. When coping with it all started to get to us, something unexpected happened. John Reed, manager of Lambright Hatchery, called and asked if White Meateor breeding stock could be purchased. I shared the request with Max; his first reaction was to ask what we were going to do with our breeder hens that had just started laying.

I contacted Cleo Lambright, the owner of Lambright Hatchery, about John Reed's request and shared some of the concerns that Max had with him. Cleo was quick to state that they would take the eggs that were left over. After all the questions were answered, we agreed to transfer the entire breeding program over to Lambright Hatchery for an agreed amount. I gave Mr. Reed a complete history on the way the White Meateor bird was developed. Number one and number two strains of birds had to be inbred and kept separate in order to get the male for cross breeding on White American breeder hens. It was a very involved program, but Mr. Reed understood what I was telling him. He told me there was no problem because he had Amish flock owners that kept small flocks who could do what was required.

Mr. Reed followed my instructions and became a very successful supplier of White Meateor chicks over the next two years, so much so that he entered a case of hatching eggs in the "Chicken of Tomorrow" contest and won first place. The tests were based on these factors: hatching percentage, livability, growth, uniformity, feed conversion, and total weight. Lambright Hatchery was selling many White Meateor chicks locally and getting orders in many other states. Mr. Reed sold inbred males to several southern hatcheries that wanted to see if the male would work with the popular Arbor-Acres and Pilch breeder hens. In both field tests, those males didn't help improve the results in the broiler houses. Eggs failed to hatch at an accepted percentage, and broiler house growth wasn't improved much. It was interesting to me that the White American breeder hens were one of the parts that contributed to making the White Meateor chicks perform in the broiler houses. Hatcheries that had other recognized breeds didn't perform with the White Meateor males. During that period, about eight strains of breeder hens were being used. The only breeder hen strain that worked great was the White American one.

In poultry genetics work, those are some of the things that show up when cross-breeding birds. When something works, it's best to stick with it. Mr. Reed kept the blood lines inbred, but when the Lambright twins returned from Pax service, the father put them in charge of the hatchery operation which had grown quite big by that time. The father suggested that the time spent on keeping those blood lines separate, in his mind, wasn't needed. He informed Mr. Reed his services were no longer required and turned over all management to Richard and Robert. They, in turn, stopped the inbreeding program and mass mated everything. In two years, they lost everything they had in terms of all the extras the White Meateor chicks had delivered. They called me one day to set up a meeting to discuss what could be done to reinstate the White Meateor benefits. They were going to bring along two college poultry geneticists that might help if they knew how I had started my program. After I explained what I had done, they both said that I did things they never heard of trying. I told them it would be impossible for me to tell how that could be fixed without starting all over. Lambright Hatchery stopped supplying White Meateor chicks and changed over to laying hen production.

Many northern Indiana broiler producers switched to egg production cage systems. They had an egg processing plant built east of the hatchery location. The loss of the White Meateor cross breed broiler blood line was most unfortunate. I should have kept a few birds separated just in case something like that should happen. I got involved in winch suspended watering and forgot about hatching White Meateor chicks for broilers. It was one of the biggest mistakes in my life because of the merits of the White Meateor cross-bred broiler chicks. It could have been possible for that cross to become the major supplier of the present day chicken sandwich.

Patent Office Experience: USA and Foreign Countries

I have had patent work done in the United States and the following foreign countries: Australia, Argentina, Belgium, Canada, England, France, Germany, Holland, India, Israel, Italy, Malaysia, Spain, and Thailand. Most of the foreign applications have been on the Ziggity watering system, and some foreign patents were on the Chore-Time auger spring feeders in France, South Africa, Belgium, and Australia. I have had my name on more than sixty-five patents in my lifetime.

In 1949, I started to develop my automatic E-Z chain driven poultry feeder and soon became aware of a need to check what patents had already been issued on such equipment, so I went to a local attorney and asked how to proceed. He told me the best legal advice was located in Indianapolis, Indiana or Chicago, Illinois. He also told me that anybody can go to the Washington D.C. Patent office to check on patents and get copies of issued patents for twenty-five cents.

My first patented invention, the E-Z Feeder, an automatic feeder system.

With that information, I decided to fly to the Washington D.C. patent office to check on automatic feeder patents. I went to South Bend, Indiana parked my car in an open field, and bought a ticket to fly to Midway Airport for eight dollars, round trip. I went to the Capital Air Lines booth, bought a round trip ticket to Washington D.C. Airport for $30, and upon arrival, took a cab to the Patent Office. How costs have changed! I asked for the automatic poultry feeder department. That involved many departments because they had no such designation as automatic poultry feeders. After some explanation, they referred me to the chain conveyor department. I spent all of my allowable time looking at all kinds of chain conveyor patents, but found nothing that pertained to feeding chickens. I did see many things that gave me added ideas on how to improve my project. I returned home safely late at night from that, my first airline business trip. I also found that I had one year of making and selling a product in the United States before I had to file a patent, but it had to be filed before a 365 day period to make the patent valid when issued. We filed in 1950 after nine months, which gave us time to install and sell many feeders. We made many improvements during that time; I included features like upstairs attachments, litter ejectors, and variable chain speed.

In July of 1950, Buckeye Incubator Company of Springfield, Ohio offered us $150,000 for complete rights to manufacture and sell the E-Z Feeder. Payment was on a royalty based on a 10% net selling price and was paid in full in three years. That was before the Nat Cortis and Gerald Kitson patent case was settled. The Mechanical Feeder Association, to which all Poultry Feeder manufacturers had to pay 10% royalties, was formed; six automatic feeder companies joined the association. The Oaks Manufacturing of Tipton, Indiana, and Jamesway of Wisconsin chose to fight the association; both went broke fighting the patent.

After eight years, Buckeye Incubator Company went bankrupt because they failed to honor customer complaints. During the first year of the Mechanical Feeder Association, they sold as many dollars worth of feeders as three of the other best manufacturers combined. That was the last year I got records because we had all of our money. I sold my interest back to the association attorney for a small sum; I wasn't interested in chain feeders anymore.

Later I started working on designing a suspended long trough waterer with an electric valve that was being tested in my breeder hen flock. I soon saw its merits and filed patents on it. I started work with a Fort Wayne firm called Lockwood, Galt, Woodward, and Smith. Maurice A. Weikart was the attorney who filed the claims. For some reason, the offices moved back to Indianapolis, Indiana. Then I went to Chicago, Illinois to the Olson, Mecklenburger, VonHolst, Pendleton, and Newman Patent Agency. I worked with Joseph Calabrese, one of the big firm's employees, and I had much trouble conveying the true merits of the suspended principal and the use of an electric solenoid valve which was combined with a Mercury switch onto a float to control hi-lo water level in the trough.

Even after many rewrites and phone calls trying to get the patent examiner to understand

Buckeye
TROUGH FOR
MECHANICAL FEEDING

DEEP HEN Trough — In actual, impartial feeding tests made by Kimber Farms, Niles, California, one of the world's leading chicken breeders, Buckeye DEEP HEN Trough saved 8.5 pounds of feed per year per layer over competitive trough designs. On 10,000 birds, this represents a solid savings profit of 85,000 pounds of feed annually. Deep Hen Trough, as the name implies, has greater depth, but in addition, greater width at the top plus down turned lip to prevent billing out. Made of 18 gauge rust resistant Zincgrip steel, it is interchangeable with any standard trough. This trough is ideal for heavy type layers, breeder hens and turkeys.

MEDIUM PULLET
Trough — Especially designed for small type layers and pullets, this trough, because of its width and depth, is relatively the same to small birds as deep trough is to heavy layers. It is the perfect trough for placing over dropping pits, slat floors, multiple roost arrangements or on floor litter. Although the newest of Buckeye trough styles, Medium is of the same solid construction as other Buckeye trough and can be used on present E-Z Feeder installations. Tests show it's the right size for small layers . . . You will save feed and money while feeding more efficiently.

BROILER Trough
Trough — Retaining the same basic design as when first introduced to the poultry industry, Buckeye BROILER Trough has maintained its popularity because it's been proved "broiler perfect." Placed at back-high-height, the side angle and lip enable birds to eat plenty, without waste . . . a profit advantage any grower appreciates. Made also of 18 gauge Zincgrip steel, this much imitated but uncopied design has been a leader in showing the advantage of mechanical over hand feeding and has helped improve conversion figures in the industry.

BROILER Trough is also available in double width (DOUBLE Trough) for extra narrow houses and in cases where hopper is located in corner feed rooms.

A copy of the promotional material used for the mechanical feeding system.

the true merits of the new suspended system, he still always based his rejection on patent claims that didn't apply.

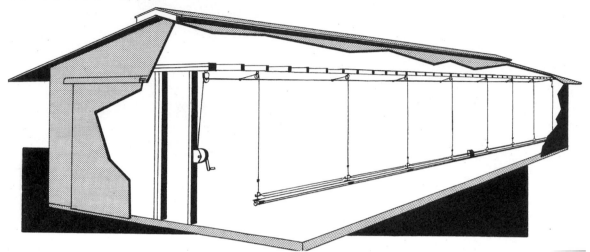

A drawing of a barn with the new suspended long trough waterer with an electric valve.

I decided to confront the examiner in person in Washington D.C. to show him the true merits of the new system. Mr. Calabrese made an appointment for me to do that, but he decided not to go with me. I found out later why he didn't go; he didn't think I was going to accomplish anything by confronting the patent examiner. I left with two sample troughs about two feet long, one with electric valves and one with a regular float. I also had a short hose with threads on both ends. Upon arrival, I asked for the examiner I had the appointment with. After a period of waiting, I was escorted to his office. After introductions, he started in to tell me why none of this was of patent merit and that the replacement of the float with an electric valve didn't merit a patent. Up to that point, I hadn't been able to get anything into the conversation other than the introduction.

I stopped him and asked where they had a janitor room to demonstrate what we had been talking about. He didn't want to talk about it any further. I told him I had brought two sets of troughs and a hose along to show the difference in the functions of the two types of systems. After a few phone calls, we were escorted to another level where a janitor room was located that had a hose threaded spigot.

We attached our hose to the electric valve equipped trough, plugged the electric cord into an outlet and, quickly, the trough was full of water. I had a siphon bulb with me, and I counted the number of bulbs full of water I had to remove from the short trough before it turned on again and refilled quickly. We then changed the hose to the float trough and let it fill up to shutoff, which took a lot longer.

I then removed a small amount of water with the siphon bulb, and small drips of water immediately started to recover water level. Then I withdrew a larger amount, which allowed a little larger amount of flow, but nothing like the electric unit. He had me hook up the electric unit again and had me draw water out until it turned on again. I told him a 100' long trough has a five gallon on/off cycle, which always attracts the birds to the trough for fresh water. During the demonstrations, he said, "Seeing is believing." He then admitted

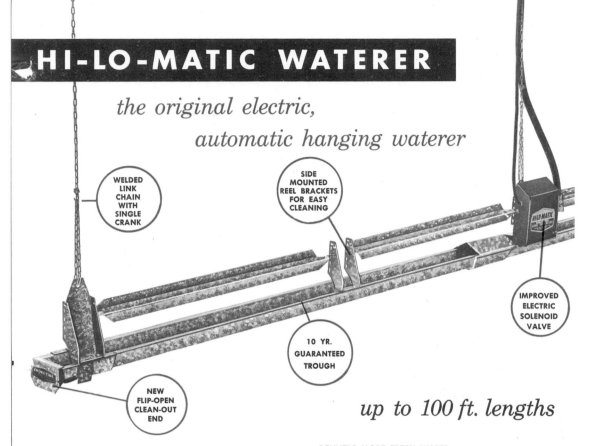

HI-LO-MATIC WATERER

the original electric,
automatic hanging waterer

WELDED LINK CHAIN WITH SINGLE CRANK

SIDE MOUNTED REEL BRACKETS FOR EASY CLEANING

IMPROVED ELECTRIC SOLENOID VALVE

10 YR. GUARANTEED TROUGH

NEW FLIP-OPEN CLEAN-OUT END

up to 100 ft. lengths

HEIGHT INSTANTLY ADJUSTABLE
Ideal for birds of all ages. One crank raises the entire trough evenly to any desired height. Now extensively used by chicken and turkey growers.

RAISES TO CEILING FOR HOUSE CLEANING
In just 60 seconds your house can be cleared for cleaning. One easy-to-operate crank raises entire length of waterer. No more rusty stand adjustments buried in litter. Trough is suspended from ceiling by chains.

NO SPILLING—NO OVERTURNED TROUGHS
The Hi-Lo-Matic is stable and will not spill even though the birds should panic and crowd It.

DELIVERS MORE FRESH WATER
A surge of fresh water moves down the trough each time the automatic valve opens. This means more profitable poultry growing. Fresh water produces more meat and more eggs. Better feed conversion is proven by tests because birds drink more fresh water.

EASY TO CLEAN
Normal surge of water keeps trough cleaner than ordinary waterers. However, when necessary to clean trough, just remove the drain plugs at each end and sweep out trough, into a bucket or dry well. Side-supported reel does not obstruct brush. Nothing to disassemble—do the job in minutes.

THE FRESH WATER PRINCIPLE

HIGH WATER LEVEL

LOW LEVEL

The illustration above shows a cross section of both high and low water levels. The difference between these levels is one filling of fresh water which you get only with the Hi-Lo-Matic electric valve.

THIS LABEL OF QUALITY
ON ALL HI-LO-MATIC GALVANIZED TROUGHS

10 YEAR GUARANTEED
TROUGH
2 OZ. EXTRA THICK
LIFE-TIME ZINC COATING

ANDERSON BOX COMPANY · INDIANAPOLIS, INDIANA
LITHO. IN U.S.A.

Promotional material used to explain the benefits of the Hi-Lo-Matic Waterer.

CHORE-MATIC®
...complete automatic poultry feeding system gives you seven profit advantages!

CHECK THESE MONEY-MAKING BENEFITS

A complete feeding system from bulk bin to bird • fresh, complete feed throughout the house • feeds at least 30% more birds per line • better feed conversion, better bird uniformity • free bird movement • ceiling suspension • wear-free, worry-free operation • no corners, no drive wheels • versatile design • two strong guarantees.

FOR FEEDING BROILERS, PULLETS, LAYERS, AND TURKEY POULTS AND BROILERS

Promotional materials used to explain the benefits of Chore-Matic's complete automatic poultry feeding system.

he hadn't understood why adding an electric valve would be an invention or make any difference.

He left the janitor's room with a totally different personality. He sat down and wrote ten new claims that he would allow on the application. I thanked him for his time and went back home, a day well spent. He called Mr. Calabrese and told him what he had done on the application after the demonstration. Mr. Calabrese couldn't believe what I had accomplished with the two samples. I didn't have any doubts after I left; it was great to hear the examiner say, "Seeing is believing." The claims were allowed soon after that meeting, and Chore-Time paid me royalties for seventeen years. The ten claims that were written by the examiner covered all functions of the winch suspended watering system. When the patent was issued on December 23, 1958, labeled number 2,865,328, it was the first patent that was issued on suspended equipment in a poultry house. The patent gave birth to a complete change in the way new poultry houses were designed. Outside curtains were put on winches, the inside heaters were placed on cables, ventilation panels were winched in cage houses. Winched straight line feeders were being asked for by the broiler growers. All poultry equipment sat on the floor in the poultry litter. That caused the stands to get rusted and it was labor intensive to adjust as birds grew. Winching equipment in a poultry house changed totally almost overnight the way broilers were managed.

When I called the Fulton Winch Company to buy winches that were designed to be used on boat trailers, the sales manager wasn't going to sell them directly to our company. After a few minutes of conversation, the owner of the company came on the phone. I told him about the new found market for boat winches, and I challenged him to a bet that the poultry industry would use more winches than the boat trailers would in the next year. The bet was that they would sell me the winches at wholesale prices. The company showed up with a display at the industry show in Atlanta, Georgia the next January. A year later, the loser would pay for the best steak dinner in Atlanta, Georgia. Guess who had a good steak one year later, courtesy of Fulton Winch Company! Each new 400' broiler house being built was equipped with this number of winches: four for outside curtains, four for feeders, sixteen for waters, and four for the heating stoves for a total of twenty-eight winches per house. An eight house complex took several hundred winches. Special winches were designed to be ceiling mounted with clutch brakes that were strong enough to hold up a 500' feeder line full of feed.

Several years later, Anderson Box Company and I started to make a hanging trough single line automatic auger feeder. Due to feed separation problems, no patents were ever made on the venture. Anderson Box Company withdrew from the project after one year. I continued with the project on my own for six months, at which time Chore-Time Equipment got involved with me again.

I had changed from a trough design project to a round hanging feeder design, and that

One of my patents.

required a special one-piece center-less spring auger to be perfected. We changed to a round feeder pan type system for feeding broiler chicks; that solved the feed separation problem we had with the trough type system. That feeder was an immediate sales success; it started to hurt chain feeder sales.

Competition started to copy the auger spring feeder in the 1960s. I was employed by Chore-Time, and they had applied for patents on the feeding system. I signed the applications and assignment of it over to Chore-Time Equipment, along with a contract to get royalties on sales. Howard decided to go to court to stop one company that fully copied the spring auger system. The patent case was assigned to Grand Rapids, Michigan because the competitor was located in that district. Chore-Time stopped paying me royalties until the case was settled. They had the contract written on the merits of the patent's legality. Chore-Time wasn't interested in my testifying in the case because I had developed the spring auger part on my own. I was asked a few questions one day by the judge concerning the functions of the total system. The judge told me before the session started that I wouldn't be asked any questions that were directed to engineering of the system because I did not have an engineering degree. The court case was into the second week when the competition decided they were going to lose. Then they decided that pulling the feed with a power unit downstream wasn't totally necessary, and that was the center of the spring auger feeder patent. They thought they could push the feed with the power unit on the hopper. They agreed to sell their systems to push feed only.

Chore-Time agreed to let them try that to get around the patent. That is why I had a sizeable royalty check when the patent case was settled after one year of no payment. I had to pay a part of the attorney costs, but all other companies that were about to enter competition on auger spring feeding systems for pulling feed were stopped. The spring worked much better pulling feed in the pipe than pushing; when pushing, the flighting would compress and expand and lock up in longer feeder lines. Chore-Time had me sign many patent applications and assignments, but only one patent case went to court while I worked there.

My next patent applications were on a closed watering system. We had good acceptance by the egg producers on our new watering system. We soon had patents issued on our first applications. When competitive watering equipment manufacturing companies saw that our product worked, they also wanted to get into the new approach. That always happens. Some companies ignore the patents and totally copy what others have made; that is what happened with the spring auger feeder. Lloyd, the president, said, "We have patents, and this has to stop". We changed to Barnes and Thornburg located at South Bend, Indiana. Dave Melton and Ryan M. Fountain prepared the depositions for an infringement suit. It became a nightmare for me because the total product was my project. The guilty company wasn't going to honor any patents or pay any royalties. When dispositions started, all my time was spent with both sets of lawyers. It involved two years of gathering information with lawyer delays before actual court action started.

During that period, the company president, Lloyd Bontrager, accompanied by his son, flew his airplane to Florida on spring break. Upon their return, they ran into bad weather "icing" that forced the plane down, and neither survived the accident. His oldest son, Wilbur, replaced him as company president of Ziggity Systems, Inc. in 1985. Larry Schrock stayed on as general manager for a period of time.

The court action on the patent case moved forward slowly. Our attorneys finally had all documents ready to go to court. We left on an airplane from South Bend, Indiana with fifteen boxes of papers. The boxes were the kind in which you store year end records. The U.P.S. delivery brought us that many more two days later. That completed the paper work they had gathered to present on the court case. We were in front of the judge for two weeks presenting our case. With both sides of attorneys taking equal time, no one seemed to enjoy what was taking place except the attorneys and the judge.

We heard nothing from the judge for many months after we returned. Costs for that type of involvement went way beyond reason. On September 27, 1990, the judge ruled our patents were valid and also awarded us damages. After many months of legal maneuvers by the infringers, they finally decided to settle in May of 1991. The regulator patent was issued, and that also became one of the issues. An agreed-to amount was added in a lump sum to cover that patent.

When the total amount of the settlement became known by Wilbur, the president, he asked Dale and me if we would consider owning the 52% that L & W Manufacturing owned. We asked them to put a price on the 52%. They came up with a price that was almost the same as the amount of the infringement check. Dale and I agreed to that, and we then owned Ziggity Systems, Inc. We had to borrow money to cover unpaid legal bills. That was paid with the next year's profits. We stopped most all patent work because of the high cost of legal action. Chore-Time Equipment sent us a notice that they had a patent issued on a small disc that retained water on the trigger pin. We had been selling turkey drinkers that had a small stainless disc with about a three-quarter inch diameter. We had found that Tom turkey's beaks got too large to get water off the disc, so we had already made plans to go to a cup-like unit that was 2½" in diameter. We signed an agreement that we wouldn't sell anymore disc type drinkers that were smaller than 2½" in diameter. This is the end of my patent experiences. Patents are a must for small companies with something new that is selling. They are crucial for keeping big companies from taking sales from others.

Chapter 12

History of Years Spent with Anderson Box Company and Chore-Time Products

During the years I was in the White Meateor Breeding and Hatching program, I lost interest in the Mechanical Chain Feeder Association, so I sold my interest back to the association manager. Later, I became interested in new types of waterers.

I started to test a cable suspended water trough that was used on my hatching egg breeders. That looked good as a new approach for raising and lowering a 100 foot long open-water trough with the turn of a winch handle. The system had an electric valve with a mercury switch attached to a float that controlled the water level in the trough. In a 100 foot trough, it had a five-gallon water differential between "on" and "off." That effect kept the trough much cleaner when it was turned on because of the rate of water flow. I had sold a number of those to broiler growers that liked them very much because they were able to raise them as the birds grew. It was also easy to raise them to the ceiling when birds were sold.

I started that project after the sale of my White Meateor breeding stock to Lambright Hatchery in 1953. Kehr Fabricated and Machine Products made some of the special parts needed to complete the trough system. After several months, the annual Poultry APHA show was held in St. Louis, Missouri. I took a demonstration model to that show, and it drew a lot of attention. Anderson Box Company got very interested in seeing how it worked in actual use in a broiler house. Jeff North, a salesman of Anderson Box Company, was most interested because of the expansion going on in his area of Texas. He brought John Holton, the president, to my booth to see the waterers demonstrated. John got interested and asked if they could be seen in operation. He came with several others, and they were all impressed after talking with broiler growers that were already using them.

Mr. Holton asked me to take the demonstration unit to Brower Manufacturing Company offices in Quincy, Illinois. That was done so all key personnel could see it and ask me all kinds of questions about its functions. I spent two days with different personnel, showing them all the features of the system. Brower Manufacturing Company was the largest supplier of broiler growing equipment to Anderson Box Company, and the salesman and John Holton didn't want to damage the relationship. Brower Manufacturing Company made stoves, floor feeders, and eight foot waters for Anderson Box Company at that time. On the last day, Bon Brower, owner of the company, came out to look at the display. He kicked the hanging trough with his foot hard enough to spill water out of it. He then said to me, "Go back and tell John Holton if he is dumb enough to try and sell this, Brower Manufacturing Company will make it when he orders it, but he needs to include full payment with the purchase order." Upon my return, I reported on Bon Brower's remarks to John Holton; John was insulted because he had seen the system installed and working.

John Holton instructed me to go see Howard Brembeck, president of Chore-Time Equipment at Milford, Indiana, to see whether he would be interested in making the new watering equipment. I took Howard, Forrest Ramser and Ken Hogan to see the broiler houses that had the waterers working. Their response was that if Anderson Box Company was interested in selling the Hi-Lo-Matic System, they were interested in manufacturing it. That was the start of the Anderson Box Company – Chore-Time Products relationship. I would be on Chore-Time's payroll and work on production and installation to train employees on winching equipment; that was an unknown to poultry equipment distributors.

That product put Chore-Time Equipment on the map quickly, and they soon outgrew their location. Howard Brembeck was sales manager of the stock tanks and hog feeders division at Star Tank and Boat Company in Goshen, Indiana. Howard Brembeck was also president of Chore-Time Equipment, Forrest Ramser was vice president, and Ken Hogan was manager of engineering. They made parts for Star Tank and Boat Company. They started in Ohio and moved to Indiana because of Howard's relationship with Star Tank and Boat Company. They had a Roll-A-Way nest, an out door feeder, and small water cup. They had started work on a basket type egg washer that Anderson Box Company started to sell after it was completed. Anderson Box Company had over thirty salesmen located across the United States selling corrugated cardboard fibre products, chick boxes, egg cases, egg cartons, feeder lids, and cardboard chick-feeders, along with the Brower Manufacturing Company's complete line of poultry products.

Anderson Box Company had a company sales meeting scheduled in the fall in Minneapolis, Minnesota. I was asked to bring the demonstration waterer setup to that meeting for all sales personnel to see and talk about. I had just purchased a new Dodge station wagon. Forrest Ramser from Chore-Time joined me on the trip with an egg washer and Roll-A-Way nest sample. I had the Hi-Lo-Matic demonstration unit with us. On the way up to Minneapolis, we listened to Perry Como sing his new hit song, "Hot Ziggity." When we got near St. Paul, Minnesota, it started to snow quite heavily, and the road soon covered with an early wet snow. A person sped past us, lost control on a curve in front of us, and went into the ditch. I had a tow strap in my Dodge, so we stopped to pull him out. We hooked one end of the loop over his bumper and looped the other end over my Dodge bumper. When I engaged the Dodge, I said, "Hot Ziggity, here we go," and we pulled him out. That is all that was said.

We proceeded to our destination and unloaded our displays. First, we had a banquet meal before the sales meeting started. They had thirty-three sales personnel and over ten office personnel at the banquet. After the meal, Forrest Ramser made his presentation on the egg washer and Roll-A-Way nest. When he was done, he spoke about how much this new venture meant to Chore-Time Equipment. He then introduced me to talk about the new Hi-Lo-Matic waterer, as "Hot Ziggity Hostetler" and told them why. That got them on their feet, and that is how I got labeled with that nickname for life. The schedule was that I was to work with every sales person to get the product installed and operating correctly. The cable suspended waterer was a totally new thing that took off like a brush fire.

The town of Milford saw that Chore-Time Equipment needed more space than was available to them at their location. The town found land that could be purchased and helped make it available at the north edge of town where Chore-Time is presently located. With the town's help, Chore-Time built a larger plant. Chore-Time Equipment grew at a rapid rate making the hanging waterers. They shipped railroad box car loads of hanging waterers to Texas from Milford. It didn't take long before broiler growers were asking for hanging feeders like the waterers.

I spoke with John Holton at Anderson Box Company to see whether they would give financial support to the development of a hanging feeder. John gave me the go ahead on the project for one year. All automatic feeders on the market at that time were endless chain feeders that sat on the floor. They had to be totally dismantled for manure removal. I had one year to make four installations on a straight line hanging feeding system.

I started with a trough shaped like a W; it had a channel with holes in it every eight inches over the center of the W for feed to drop out. The channel had a snap-on lid. I placed a specially made ten foot auger spring into the channel with a small diameter electric conduit pipe in it. The pipe had a special expansion joint attached at each end. Those joints could be expanded with set screws; that would lock the tubes and auger springs together and form a straight line auger with an internal shaft. That made up a feeding system that could be winched. The trough, channel, and auger spring combination couldn't deliver a complete feed ration the length of the system. While running, the birds would pick feed at the hole locations, thus causing fines to fall out. It proved to be a good feed separator.

I had made four installations with that type of setup; they all had the same problem. That was what I had to show Anderson Box Company at the end of the year. They stopped my support, and I was on my own with four installations that had to be improved. The customers wanted a feeder that winched. That part worked, but the feeder needed help.

It was obvious that a totally different approach was needed to make it work. I went to Delphos, Ohio and purchased enough round hanging feeders to equip one line with them in my breeder hen test house from the Delphos Manufacturing Company. I also went to

Formed Tubes, Inc. in Sturgis, Michigan, and purchased ten one-and-three-fourths inch O.D. tubes with one end swedged to go into itself. Holes were cut on opposite sides of the hanging feeder tubes about eight inches above the pan lip. The one-and-three-fourths inch diameter pipes had three holes drilled three-fourths inches in diameter for feed to drop out. The unswedged end of the pipe was inserted through the two one-and-three-fourths inch holes cut eight inches above the pan lip on opposite sides. Clamps were used to keep feeders located in position. That setup required a new hopper and motorized power unit. I removed the shafted auger spring on the W trough system. The auger springs were welded together for the 100 foot test unit. The one piece spring was inserted into the closed one-and-three-fourths inch diameter tube, the auger was attached to the 120 RPM gear motor, and the other end was anchored to the hopper bearing. That system filled the hanging feeders consecutively on the lines before going to the next. The setup made it impossible for birds to rake the feed at the discharge hole. When an obstruction that locked up the spring got into the hopper, the power unit would overpower the welds, and that would break the spring. That proved that the auger spring had to be made in one piece. The ten-foot springs I had been using were made on a lathe spring winder; that was the length one auger spring could be made.

Chore-Time saw what I was doing with my W straight line feeder. They also installed one line in Don Beer's house that was located nearby. They found the same feed separation problem with it. They tried different hole sizes and shapes with no luck before giving up. I shared with them my new approach with hanging feeders. At first, they were concerned about costs and feed waste problems with hanging feeders. They came to see how the hanging feeder was working in my breeder house; they were impressed.

My next step in the project was to try and get a one piece spring auger made on a spring winder. I made a trip to a local spring company in Mentone, Indiana. I made the mistake of asking the engineer at the location about making a one piece spring auger 500 feet long. I showed him a one-foot sample of a lathe-made auger spring. His answer was, "Any spring engineer in his right mind wouldn't even think of trying such an impossible thing. If it were possible to do it, the ideas wouldn't work because a coiled spring loaded with feed would lock up inside the tube."

I left Mentone for Logansport, Indiana, his competitor twenty miles further south. Upon arrival, I asked to see Chester Bowles the production manager. I asked if I could see how a spring winding machine worked and said that I had an application that could be used on one. He took me out into the production area and showed me all kinds of machines and different springs being made. He was soon paged for the phone.

I saw a person on a spring winder that looked as if he knew what he was doing. I showed him my sample of the lathe spring. He knew all about how my spring was made. I asked him if he could make something like that on a spring winder. He said I had a square design, which is something that isn't done on a spring winder. I asked him how long he had been employed. His answer was that he was one of the longest working employees. He told me that he worked at times on special projects to see whether they could be made. When he was told how much I would pay him personally if he could make that type of auger spring on a spring winder, he said, "I'll try it and should be able to let you know in two weeks if it's possible." I left the sample auger spring and my telephone number with him. One night about two weeks later, I received a phone call to come and see a sample auger spring made on a spring winder. I went the next day and liked what I saw. However, the machine cam cutoff allowed only eighteen feet of auger spring to be made in one piece. I told Mr. Bowles how much I liked what they had made. I asked if they could make twenty-four of those eighteen foot auger springs. Because I would weld them together to test whether they would move feed over 400 feet, Mr. Bowles agreed to let the employee make them.

He had taken a round wire and ran it between two rolls to flatten it to the same thickness and width of the sample I had left. The big problem was getting a one-and-one-half-inch pitch between coils and a one-and-one-half-inch O.D. auger spring on a spring winder. That is called a square and is a complete "no, no" on that type of machine. Mr. Bowles called me several days later and told me to pick up the auger springs. I did that and welded them together into one auger spring length 430 feet long.

I then went to Formed Tubes Inc. in Sturgis, Michigan, for enough ten feet length tubes to test whether a one piece auger spring would convey feed over 400 feet. I had to make another power unit and hopper to test the auger spring. I purchased enough electric fence posts to hang the ten foot tubes at each joint. When all was assembled and before feed was placed in the hopper, I started the motor to run the auger empty to test for amperes of current used to rotate the steel against steel in the tube when it was empty. Feed was placed in the feed hopper and run until the line was full. I then checked the amperes needed to auger feed over 400 feet. To my surprise, it took no more amperes of current to rotate the auger spring full than it did empty. The feed must have acted as a lubricant inside the tube. When the auger spring was stalled, the power

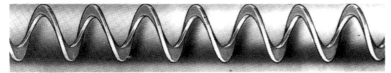

CHORE-TIME AUGER . . . STANDARD OF THE IN-DUSTRY . . . Chore-Time's straight line centerless auger mixes feed as it moves down the heavy duty galvanized metal tube to all the birds at the rate of 15 lbs. per minute. The rugged Chore-Time auger actually pulls feed which eliminates friction wear and extra horsepower required when augers push feed. So simple, effective and trouble free, is the Chore-Time manufactured auger it pulls feed on lines up to 550 feet long. There is a 10 year guarantee on the auger. Does any other manufacturer you know give such an endorsement of their equipment?

Promotional material used to market the Chore-Time Auger.

unit broke the spring at a welded point. Welding made the joints brittle.

I called Mr. Bowles and told him how great the auger spring worked moving feed 430 feet. I explained to him that welding short pieces wouldn't be acceptable because of breakage when an obstruction got into feed hoppers. I told Mr. Bowles a one piece auger spring was the answer for that application. I asked for permission to come down and help move the cam gear away from the activator arm; that would prevent the eighteen foot cutoff cycle. He set a time and date to try that with me.

They had 380 pounds of flattened wire ready when I arrived one evening after all workers had left for the day. The first task was to move the cam gear away from the activator cutoff arm. After that had been done, we soon saw that the spring winder had to be moved to another angle that formed the spring going down the aisle between other machines. We ran the auger on the floor down the aisle for eighty feet, around the corner to the next corner sixty feet, around it to the end of wire 380 feet. We found that the auger spring weighed one pound per feet of auger spring. They used rotating tables to feed wire into the machines. One had a three foot diameter table. We used it to coil the auger spring back onto it. It was amazing how nice the coils stacked on top of each other. The 380 feet of each winding was only increased one-fourth inch in height by the width of the wire. I loaded the coil of wire in the back of my station wagon and went home.

I knew that this was the biggest new thing I would ever accomplish in my life. That one piece square design auger spring has proven to be the most efficient method of feeding poultry, hogs, and cattle in the world.

I placed the one piece auger in my backyard setup and ran feed to the end with no problem. I then placed a foreign object into the feed hopper to stall the one-eighth H.P. motor to see what happened to the auger spring. The auger spring stalled the motor when the overload button tripped the motor off. When it spun back at an extreme high speed, the centrifugal starting switch was destroyed in the motor, and I knew then that the power unit couldn't damage the auger spring. The things needed to overcome the spin back problems were going to be very simple to overcome.

At that point, I went back to Chore-Time to let them know about the one piece auger spring. They became interested in getting involved in some way since Anderson Box had left the project. Both Anderson Box Company and Chore-Time were busy selling and making Hi-Lo-Matic waters. The next step in the feeder design was to get a cone designed that could be attached to the one-and-three-fourths O.D. feeder tube.

Chore-Time had given up on Don Beer's trough feeders and wanted to change his line over to a tube hanging feeder system. Larry Myers called the engineering department of the spring company about ordering a spring for the Don Beer house. The engineer told him they wouldn't think of trying something like that. That started a chain of reaction that came all the way back to me. I made an appointment to meet with the president of

Mullenhauser Spring Company to resolve the problem. I left with my Buckeye Incubator Company royalties records and showed him potential sales in automatic poultry feeder sales. I was able to convince the president to go forward on the project, and I told him why I had to do it the back door way. He called the manager of engineering into the meeting to tell him about his decision to make auger springs. The engineer tried to defend his earlier decision and said he couldn't see how anybody could have come into their company and got past engineering on such a big project with no one in engineering knowing about it. They made many thousands of miles of auger springs for Chore-Time Equipment Company before Chore-Time started to make them themselves.

Larry Myers had designed a special cone that attached to the feeder line tube. Chore-Time purchased a sixteen inch diameter round hanging feeder pan from Cyclone Manufacturing Company, Urbana, Indiana. The pans were made to be adjustable for different feeds. The cone feeder system was called Mono-line hanging feeder system. It also became an instant sales success due to the hanging straight line feature to raise and lower with a winch. It opened up the broiler houses to bird movement without having to get across endless feed troughs on the floors. The first big improvement on that system was a need to have a grill to keep older birds from wasting feed out of the cone type feeder setup. We had many of those installed in all parts of the United States. Most growers liked the system but wished that older birds couldn't get into the feeder pans. That required

Promotional material used to market the Chore-Time Monoline Poultry Feeder.

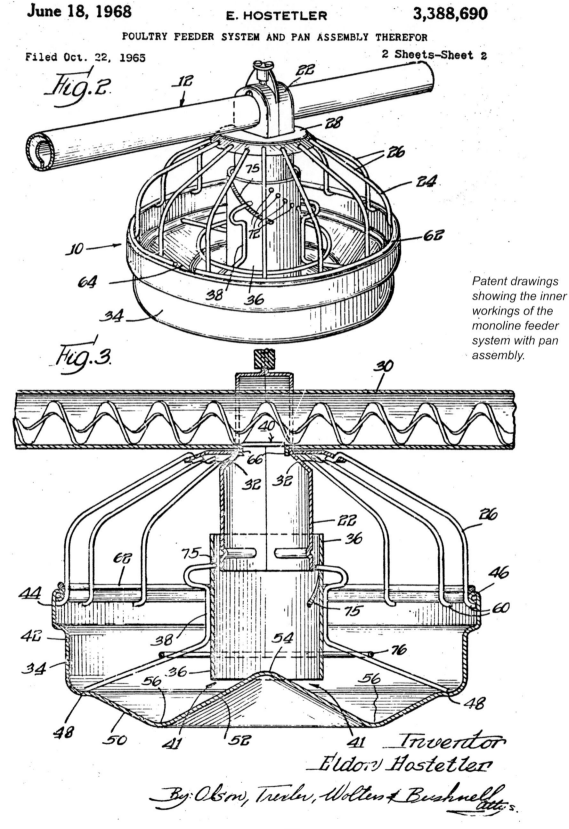

June 18, 1968   E. HOSTETLER   3,388,690

POULTRY FEEDER SYSTEM AND PAN ASSEMBLY THEREFOR

Filed Oct. 22, 1965   2 Sheets—Sheet 2

Fig. 2

Fig. 3

Patent drawings showing the inner workings of the monoline feeder system with pan assembly.

Inventor
Eldon Hostetler
By: Olson, Trexler, Wolters & Bushnell
Attys.

complete redesign of the pan assembly. Keeping birds out after they were several weeks old required a grill over the pan. We then designed a smaller diameter pan. We also made a much smaller capacity feeder reserve cone and made the assembly to swing freely on the pipe. That model was completed in the fall of 1962 but was advertised as model 63 grill feeder. The feeder assembly held much less feed and was well accepted by the industry.

It became an important project to design an overhead ceiling mount winch that could handle a 500 feet feeder line with a one-half H.P. drill powered by electricity or air. Several worm gear units were made, but they failed with lines full of feed or were just too slow.

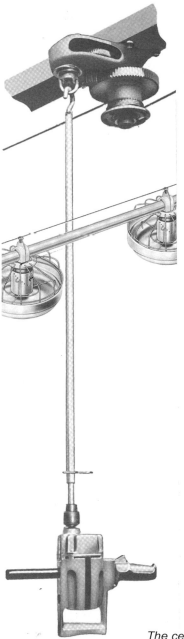

Dale Marshal and I worked on a spur gear driven winch that could be ceiling mounted. We added a self-braking clutch that held at any stopped location. That made it possible for a one-half H.P. electric or air drill to lift a 500 foot feeder line full of feed. The ceiling mounted winch had to be located at the center of a 500 foot feeder line overhead. The winch was mounted on a two inch by eight inch wide plank that was twelve feet long. That plank was then nailed to the overhead rafters at a 250 foot location. That setup made it easy for the broiler grower to raise his feeder and water lines as the birds grew. It also made it easy to lift the lines to the ceiling so the catching crew could move catching crates into the building close to bird locations. That cut catching and walking time by a large percentage.

Howard asked me to try to make an automatic cage feeder that worked in present day cage troughs, troughs that were hand fed with person-driven feed carts that fed two levels on the same side. That became a mountain of a project that just got higher as it went. The project started in a big Pockman cage house on U.S. 20 near Middlebury, Indiana. We placed a special close pitch auger spring in the trough; the close pitch added weight so that rotation didn't lift the auger up on top of the feed. That worked but required much longer running time to complete a feeding cycle. We dropped that approach due to running time and feed distributors.

We next placed a standard auger in our one-and-three-fourths inch broiler pipe on top of a cage row at Vernon Bontrager's house near New Paris, Indiana. The pipe had holes at alternate cage partitions; located at the holes were

The ceiling mounted winch system used to lower and raise the feeding system.

two inch square drops down into the open trough. That had great promise, but during the first week, the birds were afraid when it ran and didn't eat. During the second week, they started to rake feed away from the drop during running and overloaded the troughs with feed. After three weeks, the system was removed due to failure to control feed level in the troughs.

We then made a special smaller auger one-and-one-eighth inch O.D. with one inch pitch that ran in a one-and-one-fourth inch O.D. tube. We removed the open feed trough on one cage row. We replaced it with six inch wide feed cups with feed level baffles. The cups were located at alternative partitions. They were attached to the one-and-one-fourth inch tube located in front of cage row, where the continuous open trough was located. The tubes had an outlet hole at alternate cage partitions for feed to be deposited in the cup. That system required keeping the right number of birds in the last cage, where the shutoff control cup was located. We had several cage houses equipped with that type of system that worked quite well. Some birds would regurgitate water into the galvanized cups, and that would form mold and cause birds to get sick. If those cups had been made of plastic, there wouldn't have been a problem. Some of those cup cage houses lasted several years before a flock of hens regurgitated, causing it to fail.

We then started with the small auger placed in an open channel located in a special designed trough. The open top channel was located inside the front of the trough, facing the birds when eating. When the hens raked feed away from the channel holes, it piled up. When that happened, it would fall into the open top channel and move on down the line. That type of system worked with close management. The feed had to be ground real fine so as to remove all efforts of feed separation. We tried adjustable channels and different hole shapes and sizes before the product was no longer sold.

The last thing I tried was to shape a trough with a round bottom to the size of the 1½" spring auger. That auger was rotated at eighty R.P.Ms per minute. I had several of those setups running in the area that worked well in two-level cages. That system was dropped due to the mechanism required to make it work on all applications. The last thing tried and still being used is the round bottom trough design with angled open sides. Instead of rotating the auger to move feed, it pulls it. Several power units with drive sprockets were placed on a long circuit, and it worked like a chain feeder.

Howard called me into his office, asking what I knew about progress on the adult turkey feeder. That wasn't my project at that point. I told him I heard they had many problems with the big turkeys damaging what they tried. The project manager was trying to strengthen the standard wire grill broiler feeder assembly to withstand adult turkey abuse with no success. He asked me to get involved because of lack of current progress. He then asked me what plans I had that would work. The plans I had were only in my head at that time. I told him if he wanted me to be responsible for a working adult turkey feed,

I would need complete freedom to do what the job would take. I also told him the feeder would be more costly to make, but it would work. He gave me his consent, so I went to work on the adult turkey feeder. First, I ordered 2" O.D. pipes with a wall heavy enough to do one line in the Pine Manor house. I then went to All Metal Spinners, Angola, Indiana, to get spun a new design cover shield and turkey feeder pan. I had four special steel straps made for each cover pan assembly unit. The steel straps were long enough to allow adult

CHORE-TIME®

Adult Turkey Confinement Production Systems

Promotional material used to market the adult turkey feeding system.

turkeys to access their heads for feed. The total assembly consisted of the following parts: a 2½" square drop tube with two holes for the 2" O.D. feeder tube to be inserted through a circular cone with adjusting holes, feed adjusting wire stand, pan cover, four metal support straps, and feed pan.

The wire grilled turkey feeder line was removed at the Pine Manor turkey house. In its location, we installed the new style turkey feeder with a cover over the feeder pan. The cover was added to protect the pan because turkeys often jump into the air and sometimes fail to clear equipment when landing. It was soon determined that the adult

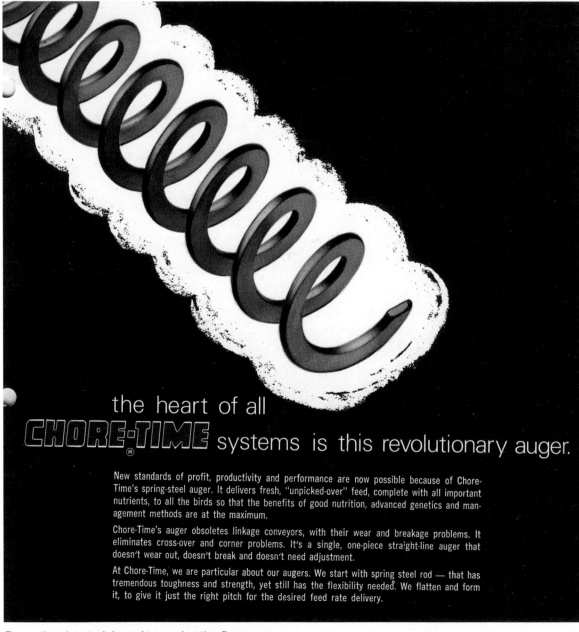

the heart of all CHORE-TIME® systems is this revolutionary auger.

New standards of profit, productivity and performance are now possible because of Chore-Time's spring-steel auger. It delivers fresh, "unpicked-over" feed, complete with all important nutrients, to all the birds so that the benefits of good nutrition, advanced genetics and management methods are at the maximum.

Chore-Time's auger obsoletes linkage conveyors, with their wear and breakage problems. It eliminates cross-over and corner problems. It's a single, one-piece straight-line auger that doesn't wear out, doesn't break and doesn't need adjustment.

At Chore-Time, we are particular about our augers. We start with spring steel rod — that has tremendous toughness and strength, yet still has the flexibility needed. We flatten and form it, to give it just the right pitch for the desired feed rate delivery.

Promotional material used to market the flex auger.

turkeys weren't going to hurt the system at any time. That design is still being used by Chore-Time Equipment and its competitors today.

Outside bulk feed bins were made available to poultry farmers at that time. The bins were equipped with four-inch auger and universal joints where any change in direction was needed with those shafted auger systems. The universals had a custom of breaking after short usage under loaded conditions.

Chore-Time Equipment had made a 3" O.D. shafted circulating system to maintain feed in feeder line intake cups. That system consisted of these parts: an inside feed hopper, two 90 degree cast corners (one unpowered, one with ½ H.P. motor unit), and a parallel return box with spur gears. Drops from their overhead system kept feed in the intake feed cups below as long as feed was kept in the feed supply hopper.

I saw the way the cost of all this mechanism might be removed from the feeding system. At that point, the industry had no method other than shafted augers to move feed in closed tubes larger than 2". Chore-Time Equipment had 3" O.D. pipes they supplied with their shafted 2½" augers.

My thoughts were: Why not try to make an auger spring to go around a 90 degree corner in a 5' radius with a 3" O.D. pipe? The need was coming for something just like that directly out of the bulk feed bin. That would make location of bulk feed supply bins much more flexible. The 9' piece of pipe bent in a 5' radius could be cut to accommodate any angle out of the bin. Most all bins on the market were 6' diameter side draw, 6' center draw, and 9' center draw. I had wood overhead bins in my own chicken house at that time with slide shutoff.

I went to the engineering department at Mullenhauser Spring Company in Logansport, Indiana to see whether they would be interested in helping me get a sample spring made on a spring winder. I needed a 110' long spring from the bulk feed bin to the six feed hoppers inside the 110' wide poultry house. That time, engineering was glad to help on the trial test. They tried several different diameter wires flattened to different widths before they thought they had something to try. During that period, I had Steury Boat Company make me the first 30 degree fiberglass Flex-auger boot to be attached to an outside bulk collar bin. The boot had a bearing anchor for maintaining a small tension on the auger if full or empty of feed. The power unit was located at the last drop inside the building. The spring company made a 2½" O.D. flex auger 110' long to go into my fill system. The first augers broke in the elbows in only a short period of usage. I welded them together; however, they broke again in several days. They made the wire thinner and wider and made the pitch a little closer; that auger ran well and lasted. We started right away to get a 3½" O.D. auger to work in the 4" Flex auger system. That size would require much less running time to keep inside hoppers full. Several more sizes have been added to supply the market needs.

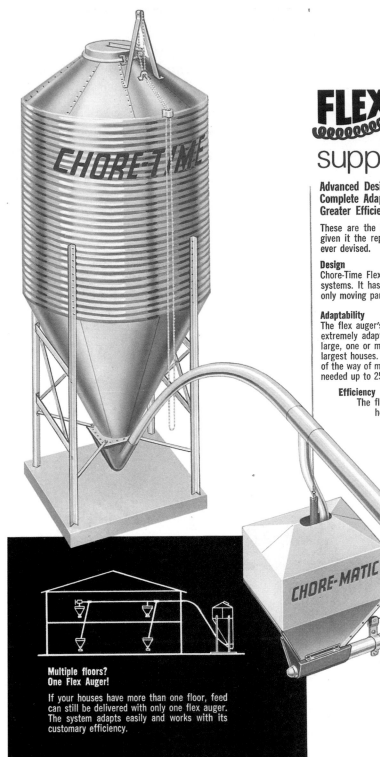

FLEX AUGER®
supply system

Advanced Design
Complete Adaptability
Greater Efficiency

These are the hallmarks of the Flex Auger System which have given it the reputation as being the best feed conveying means ever devised.

Design
Chore-Time Flex Auger eliminates many problems found in other systems. It has a patent protected design to pull the feed. The only moving parts are one motor and a one-piece flex auger.

Adaptability
The flex auger's ability to convey feed in any direction makes it extremely adaptable to most any type of poultry house, small or large, one or more floors. It has the capacity to supply even the largest houses. The feed conveying tube is easily mounted up out of the way of men and machinery. It can be supplied in any length needed up to 250 feet.

Efficiency
The flex auger delivers up to 2400 pounds of feed per hour with only one horse power motor operating at 328 RPM making its operational cost the lowest. Feed is kept fresh in the closed tube and because of the cradling action of the flex auger, feed consistency is not impaired.

Multiple floors?
One Flex Auger!

If your houses have more than one floor, feed can still be delivered with only one flex auger. The system adapts easily and works with its customary efficiency.

Promotional material used to explain the benefits of the flex auger supply system.

The 20 years that I was involved with Chore-Time Equipment were a great help to me in learning how to deal with the public. Howard and I had a great relationship. We somehow knew what we expected from each other without saying anything. Howard, like me, knew that the customer was always right even if we both knew internally that was not always the case. Howard most always gave me compete freedom to do what I thought might work on a product design. If it didn't, I knew that he expected me to make it work without his telling me how it should be done.

When you see the way a company that started in a small town like Milford, Indiana having only three persons making mostly parts for Star Tank and Boat Company in Goshen, Indiana grew in fifty short years to be owned by Warren Buffett, you know that company knew what the customer needed and wanted. Warren Buffett knew why he needed a company like Chore-Time Equipment to build on. The twenty years I had with Chore-Time Equipment helped me to work with many different kinds of problem personnel complaints. Ken Hagens was one of the owners of Chore-Time Equipment and was in charge of engineering. He soon left the company because the fast growth of the company overwhelmed him.

Larry Myers was hired from New Holland, Pennsylvania to help in engineering to replace Ken Hagens. Larry also found himself almost overwhelmed at times with all the new things Chore-Time was introducing to the poultry and swine industry. That was being done at a rate never seen before, and was being done very successfully.

I am pleased that I had a part in the period when all this was taking place. I want to thank the Lord for giving me the opportunity to be alive in a day and age when so many things were possible.

In the United States, one hundred, seventy million six week-old broiler birds are killed in processing plants every week, mostly for chicken sandwiches. They are all fed with the special spring auger that I had the persistence to get past all engineers who knew that, even if it could be made, it wouldn't work in a closed tube full of feed! Manufacturers of poultry equipment located all over the world copied the auger spring feeder design after the patent expired in 1975.

Laying houses and broiler houses are getting bigger every year. The auger spring is being made in ever longer lengths, up to over 600 feet long to cover those needs. If combining the total world's weekly production with that of the United States, a total of over three million broilers would be processed every week. It is a very popular meat for a quick sandwich and is healthful for the body.

It gives me great satisfaction that I inherited a trait that encouraged me to "never give up on something that is truly needed." I persisted in that goal in creating an endless spring auger after being told that it couldn't be done. Even if it could be done, I heard over and over, somehow it wouldn't work inside a closed tube full of feed. Sometimes not having an engineering degree helps. My father taught me that "*a quitter never wins and a winner never quits.*"

I resigned my position at Chore-Time Equipment at Milford, Indiana after my wife was diagnosed with breast cancer in 1975. In 1977, she lost her battle with cancer after eighteen months. I then started Ziggity Systems, Inc., manufacturing a closed pipe watering system.

One of the many laying houses set up across the United States that supply the eggs for the egg market across the country.

Chapter 13

The History of Ziggity Systems, Inc.

In October of 1975, Edna and I went to Germany to visit Dale and wife Pam for two weeks. He was stationed there in the service. We traveled to many different places, including Switzerland, Denmark, and Sweden. Upon our return, Edna drove her parents to Florida in November and stayed two weeks. During that period, I sent Chore-Time a letter of resignation effective January 1, 1976. I planned to make a new cage cup drinker.

When Edna returned, she confirmed to me that she might have a serious health problem; her left arm and breast had started to swell. I had already done a doctor's examination for insurance coverage before she returned. We made appointments to have her health problems checked. All tests and x-rays failed to show any problems. We then had a breast biopsy done at the hospital. Edna was told that if she came out of recovery with her breast intact, she could be sure she didn't have cancer; however, they didn't tell her that tissues had to be sent to a lab for testing. A day later, the doctor walked into her room and reported that the lab report indicated her breast needed to be removed. She went into total hysteria, and I failed to be with her at that moment. I had gone to my parents to report that the biopsy had not shown cancer tissues. Upon my return, doctors were preparing her for breast removal because of a very rare type of cancer. The procedure wasn't done until into 1976 because of the doctors' failure to find cancer sooner.

I spent most of my time with her while doctors did tests and took x-rays trying to determine what was giving her so much pain. After the breast was removed, she had some relief of her pain, and it started to heal nicely. The doctors didn't give her much information on her kind of cancer or of what she might expect. I wasn't going to push them because they said they didn't know much about it, and that they had never seen a breast with her kind of cancer. It had already spread to her arm, and that was giving her a lot of pain. The doctors told me a healing miracle was the only thing that could save her life, and that ninety days could be all she had left. Edna had such a desire for life and for conquering cancer that her cancer went into a period of remission.

During that period, I worked on designing a self-filling cage cup. Bender Mold and Machine, Inc. in Mishawaka, Indiana, made single cavity molds for sample plastic parts for testing. I showed the cup to several cage egg producers and got very negative reports. They all said the need for another cup wasn't there. John Frederich, manager of Creighton

Brothers, Inc., Warsaw, Indiana advised me to make a nipple type drinker that snapped into a saddle like all cups did. That required changing all the tooling to a new design that was done by keeping the valve mold and saddle mold and converting them into a nipple type that would snap into a saddle. All nipples on the market were threaded into a heavy wall plastic pipe. When removed for cleaning, it was almost impossible to get them reinstalled because of cross-threading; they would leak, and that required replacing the pipe. I placed a line of the nipple drinkers with my breeder hens and found the hens using them. I used the only regulator that was available — one made in New Zealand. When it was adjusted to very low pressure, a very low flow of water went through it. It was obvious that regulator wouldn't work on water lines over 100 feet in length.

I asked Dick Bender, owner of Bender Mold, if he would let me use his lathe to try and make a seven inch diameter aluminum regulator. I had no drawing, just plans in my head. I purchased a seven inch diameter round bar six inches long and cut off two pieces 2¾" thick. I started machining the parts being held together around the outside with nine bolts and with a rubber diaphragm between the two parts. Internal parts consisted of reduction arm, rubber seat inlet orifice, and backing plate fastened to the center of the diaphragm. That unit had a twelve inch plastic see-through stand pipe with a floating blue ball to check outlet water pressure. After three days of machining and one day of assembling, the time came for testing whether it would work. It did beyond our fondest dreams! It could be adjusted down to one inch pressure. Twenty-eight inches of water in a vertical stand pipe equals one pound of water pressure. I then used the regulator and enough parts with single cavity molds to put one line of three-fourth inch galvanized floor pipe in Creighton Brothers' starter pullet house that was 250 feet long. That was the start of the Ziggity Systems, Inc. snap-in nipple type drinker.

I saw that the new nipple system could work and be sold, so I checked with the county offices to see if I could use my 12,000 square foot chicken house to make the system. They asked if that required semi-trucks to travel on county roads. It was going to require trucks for

The Ziggity-Flo Regulator

bringing and taking products. The officials responded that no new operations were going to be allowed to start on county roads because of road damage. They advised me to get into an industrial park location. Lloyd Bontrager, President of Jayco Manufacturing, had purchased a piece of land located across the road from the Jayco offices that was made into industrial parks. Middlebury Electric had built and used the 40′ X 100′ building several years but had outgrown it and had moved to the Goshen area. It was a pole building with three offices in the front. I asked Lloyd about renting it for making a product. His first question concerned the product I was making. I told him it was a new drinker system. His next question was, "Where can I see it?" I showed him a sample. "Have you tested it yet?" I told him I had it installed in my test house at home. He told me I wasn't the first to inquire about renting the building. "Whoever gets it will be in a partnership with me on my terms." He wanted to see what the system in my house looked like. He came and looked, then informed me he would contact me before he planned anything with any other party. I wasn't looking for a partnership at that moment and decided to look around more. Dick Dalhstrom, who was going to be sales manager, drove with me to several industrial parks to see whether anything was available. We found land available to build on but no empty buildings.

We went back to Lloyd and asked what the terms were going to be. His answer was he had to have several days to think about it, that it might be with L & W Engineering Company which belonged to Lloyd and his son Wilbur. L & W made parts for the lift system on fold-down campers for Jayco. Lloyd called several days later to tell me his terms for a partnership setup. They were thus: L & W Engineering was an S Corporation and was going to own 80 percent until there were two years of profit conjoint of several thousand dollars. When that happened, it would revert 52 percent to L & W and 48 percent to Dick, Dale, and me. We were asked to put up $20,000 to match their amount in the startup fund. Dick Dalhstrom put up $8,100, and I did the rest, including Dale's share. Lloyd was going to hire a manager who also had accounting skills; his salary and rent would be charged against the operation.

The original building for Ziggity Systems, Inc. located on State Highway 13 across from Jayco.

I had already spent $75,000 to bring a product to the present point, and I asked how I was going to get repaid for those efforts. Patents were brought into the conversation at that point, and Lloyd wanted to know if anything could be patented. He asked if I would go with him to his patent attorney in South Bend, Indiana and meet Eugene C. Knoblock. We met, and Mr. Knoblock assured us that patents could be issued on the new watering system. Lloyd assured me that a royalty percentage on sales would help me recapture my investment.

My daily morning routine at that time was to help Edna get dressed and to place the pain blocking attachment on her arm and shoulder. The unit was used at St. Joseph Hospital to block her pain. When she was ready to leave the hospital, they weren't going to let me take it along. After agreeing to pay for it, they allowed me to take it. At first, it helped a great deal. It had four batteries that lasted twelve hours, and four batteries were always in the charger for the next period. The unit was adjustable and helped keep her pain controlled. On April 22, 1977, Edna succumbed to her battle with rare cancer. After the funeral, I took time to take care of the things that needed to be taken care of.

However, life goes on, so I tried best as I could to go ahead with plans that were started. I worked with the patent attorney to get all the new features on our system covered. We were going to need eight cavity molds on all plastic parts. On the drinker, those included: drinker body, cap, seat, saddle, and pipe connectors. The regulator was going to be two molds, one mold top half and bottom half, and internal parts in the other mold. The eyelet and trigger pin were custom made of stainless steel. The five-sixteenth inch diameter stainless steel ball was standard. The three-fourths inch galvanized pipe being used for floor systems was standard size pipe purchased 1.050 O.D. in different lengths.

To get plastic molds made, we had to make down payments to Bender Mold and Machine. We went to Jayco's company bank in 1977 and borrowed $125,000 at twenty-one percent interest. That was to cover the down payment cost on seven molds that had to be completed before an installation could be made; that was going to take six months to complete. I kept working with Mr. Knoblock on getting a registered name for the company; but all the names I suggested were already registered. Dick Dalhstrom suggested checking to see whether my nickname, Ziggity, was registered. It was not, so we added "Systems, Incorporated" with it and placed an oval circle around the words. When Knoblock had that completed, we started our company on April 29, 1977.

Ziggity Systems, Inc. logo, designed for the start of the company, April 29, 1977.

Molds that made it possible to install our first cage house for Jack Anglin at Clunnette Elevator in late November were completed in November. In January 1978, we did a big cage house near Mentone, Indiana for Creighton Brothers. Creightons had a big Open House program before birds were placed. Cage operators came from great distances to see the cage house and equipment, and that helped us sell more installations. At that point, we had no broiler houses using our cage drinkers. We had a floor system that was being used in starting pullet chicks that were to be transferred to laying cages. Producers wanted drinker systems that were alike so birds wouldn't die because they lacked water when they were transferred to cages.

The number of birds needed to supply eggs for the United States is much smaller than the numbers needed in the broiler industry. In the United States, 170,000,000 broilers are processed every week; birds are only six weeks old when processed. In order to replace the houses with new chicks, 190,000,000 eggs are placed in the incubators every week. That requires enough special cross-bred hens in layer houses laying eggs weekly to supply them; those birds also need a clean drink. It can be seen that the poultry meat production system is where the drinker sales are. Burnett Poultry in Jamestown, Tennessee, was the first to try our system on broilers and found much less bird sickness because each bird was getting water out of a closed pipe system. On a closed system, each bird has to trigger the pin to release water from the overhead pipe into its mouth. The merits of the system spread quickly throughout the industry. Stan Lowery of Watkinsville, Georgia was growing birds for Central Soya, and Marvin Green was operations manager. Stan Lowery had just purchased a six house operation; the houses were 36′ x 400′ buildings. I asked them for permission to install one house for test purposes, and they said I had to get approval from Marvin Green. I did meet with Marvin and got him convinced to do one house. I promised to help install the test house at Stan Lowery's. When the installation was complete, the chicks from the hatchery were delivered.

The Big Z Breeder System waterers shown in use.

The driver and helper looked at the watering system and said we couldn't unload the chicks until some adequate watering means were supplied. I was at the farm when they made the statement. They were told that this was going to be a test against the other five houses. They were ready to bet money that this house wasn't going to win, because the chicks wouldn't find the water, and many would die. They called the hatchery and told them what was going on and asked whether they should unload; they were told to check with Marvin Green to see whether he, indeed, agreed to go along with the test. They had serious doubts about the way their 16,000 chicks would find a drink because they had never seen anything like this method before. Most all broiler houses were equipped with an open v-type water trough that chicks could see into. Marvin told them to take one box of chicks to the far end of the broiler house and place them near the waterline and watch what happened, then report back to him. The man at the hatchery was just as concerned as the driver was. They took the one box of chicks and placed them per Marvin's instruction. Before they had all of them placed, the first ones were already crowding to get at the drinkers. The men stood and watched a few minutes. The driver said, "I never saw anything like this before in my life. Let's unload; if I didn't see it I wouldn't believe it."

Promotional material used to share the advantages of the floor watering system with E-Z sip drinkers.

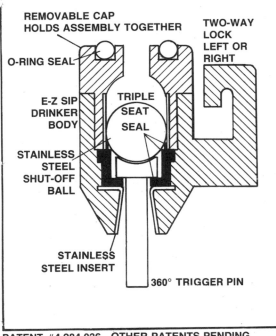

THE E-Z SIP DRINKER

REMOVABLE CAP
HOLDS ASSEMBLY TOGETHER

TWO-WAY
LOCK
LEFT OR
RIGHT

O-RING SEAL

E-Z SIP
DRINKER
BODY

TRIPLE
SEAT
SEAL

STAINLESS
STEEL
SHUT-OFF
BALL

STAINLESS
STEEL INSERT

360° TRIGGER PIN

PATENT #4,284,036   OTHER PATENTS PENDING

That house had the least death loss in starting. The noise from the drinkers being activated by the click attracts the other day-old birds. That is why the system became an instant success story in broiler production world wide. The results from that test opened all of Georgia to our drinker system. Today, Georgia is the largest broiler producing state in the United States; it uses our drinker in most broiler production houses.

On April 8, 1978 I married a lady that I promised to love and cherish the rest of my life. Her name was Esta May Yoder. We had a combination honeymoon and working trip to Australia and New Zealand. We stopped first in Hawaii for three days, then on to

New Zealand for two days, then overnight to Australia. I worked installing watering equipment the first two days near Sidney. The next several days were spent in sales work at different locations. We than flew to Perth and met with salespersons for one day. We were told to stop in Singapore for several days, which we did. That must be the nicest place on earth! We have been many places and found nothing cleaner or more attractive.

We started to have problems with seat material; we were told that A.B.S. (Acrylonitrile-Butadiene-Slyrene) and P.V.C. (Poly Vinyl

April 8, 1978, wedding photo when I married Esta May (Yoder) Hostetler.

Chloride) material with Plastizer added to the P.V.C. for softening is not compatible. We then changed the seat to a Shell product called Kraton because it was believed that A.B.S. and Kraton don't react to each other.

At that time, Dick Dalhstrom and Lloyd, the president of Ziggity agreed to disagree; Dick left, and he wanted his money out of Ziggity Systems, Inc. I was instructed by Lloyd to take care of that, so I refunded his money, over $8,000. Robert Hostetler came back from school in Sweden and asked if he could take Dick's place in sales. It wasn't long before he asked to have stock in the company. I told him that no stock had been issued because of our setup. At that point, I had paid in all of the promised forty-eight percent ownership until two years of profit had occurred. I told Robert I had no stock or anything because, at that point, L & W owned 80% of the total ownership. I had signed a paper stating that I had no right to do anything with my interest before I told L & W. That was a major thorn in Robert's mind, and he didn't accept it as valid.

In 1980, we did a complete change in the design of the drinker. We went to a 360 degree concave trigger pin, a stamped eyelet, and a new seat design. We didn't have any money to operate after those things were done; soon after that, the bank called our loan. That instantly caused a big problem for continuing operations. The L & W owners weren't too concerned because the RV industry was also down to almost nothing. I checked with several banks with Larry Schrock, L & W's company manager. They were all more concerned with what was happening in the RV industry. We heard about a startup bank in Elkhart, Indiana called Citizen Bank that was looking to help small startup companies that needed help; we thought

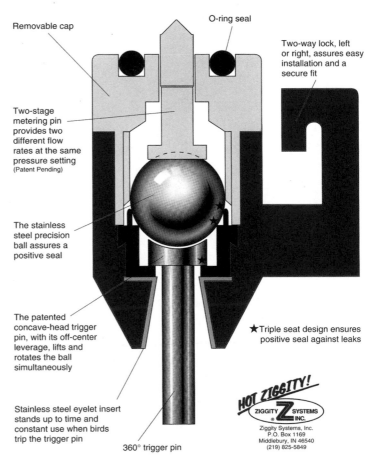

The 1400 E-Z Sip Drinker

Removable cap

O-ring seal

Two-way lock, left or right, assures easy installation and a secure fit

Two-stage metering pin provides two different flow rates at the same pressure setting (Patent Pending)

The stainless steel precision ball assures a positive seal

The patented concave-head trigger pin, with its off-center leverage, lifts and rotates the ball simultaneously

★Triple seat design ensures positive seal against leaks

Stainless steel eyelet insert stands up to time and constant use when birds trip the trigger pin

360° trigger pin

HOT ZIGGITY!
ZIGGITY **Z** SYSTEMS INC.
Ziggity Systems, Inc.
P.O. Box 1169
Middlebury, IN 46540
(219) 825-5849

Promotional material used to show the advantages of the E-Z Sip Drinker.

we should qualify if that was their goal. We did check them out and offered to take them to our operation and to installations using our systems. After several days, they came back with a report as to what they could offer us if L & W and I did thus and so. I was greatly encouraged and ready to do what they asked. They gave us this report: we will take care of the loan balance of the original loan if L & W and each of us put in $75,000; that would give us enough money to operate. I went to my bank and borrowed $75,000 on my home to put into Ziggity Systems, Inc. operations. I told Larry Schrock what I was going to do with the understanding that part of the money would be used to buy an E.P.D.M. rubber seat mold with 495 cavities from Minnesota Rubber Company. The mold was going to cost $3,995 and take eleven weeks to complete. That kept things going.

After several weeks, I got a phone call from the Citizen Bank president asking me when I was coming in to sign the loans that were ready for signature. I told him I had already put my $75,000 into Ziggity Systems, Inc., and he wasn't very happy about that because they hoped to do my loan. He was quick to tell me that the whole deal was off if I didn't sign both the L & W Engineering and Ziggity loan. I told him I thought the signature of the president of Ziggity was all that was needed; however I went and signed the two loans. We got our seat mold quicker and started to use E.P.D.M seats, and all things changed for the better. We had to replace many seats in drinkers, but sales were so strong that we started making a good profit. We had to operate nine hours a day for five and a half days a week to keep up with sales. We shipped most all orders in bulk packaging. In two years, I had my loan paid off and had made profits that were ready to change ownership to 52 percent and 48 percent. In three years, we had the bank paid off. During that period, Robert decided to leave and form a company with a friend in Holland where they would sell our drinker under a different name. He had a good amount of success until competition started.

In the fall of 1980, we saw the need of a multiple punching system. We set up a new multiple hole punch for all of these 6", 8", 10", 12", 15", 16", 18", 20", 24", 30", 32" 36", 40", and specials. Pipe lengths to do those spacing were 8', 9' and 10' for cages; for floor systems, they are mostly ten foot pipes. For floor systems, we were using three-fourths inch galvanized pipe with a special two piece clamp to seal around the drilled hole in galvanized pipe. We stopped doing that because of rust problems inside the pipe. We used parts of the bracket to clamp around the galvanized pipe to support the plastic that was placed directly under the galvanized pipe for support. The water was then directed to the bird by the plastic pipe under the galvanized pipe which was there for support only. Up to that point, all saddles and attachments were glued onto the A.B.S. pipes. Cage layer operations were looking at start-grow cages to grow replacement pullets. All that was available were Hart cups. If they had nipple type drinkers in laying houses, bird loss could result because birds could not find water.

We were asked to come up with a system to water chicks in a cage at a day old. That

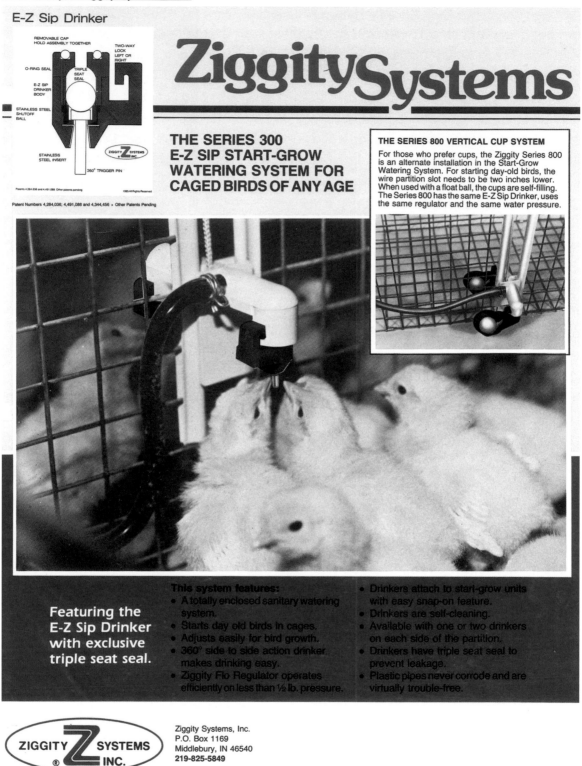

E-Z Sip Drinker

REMOVABLE CAP
HOLD ASSEMBLY TOGETHER

TWO-WAY
LOCK
LEFT OR
RIGHT

O-RING SEAL

TRIPLE
SEAT
SEAL

E-Z SIP
DRINKER
BODY

STAINLESS STEEL
SHUTOFF
BALL

STAINLESS
STEEL INSERT

360° TRIGGER PIN

Patents 4,284,036 and 4,491,088 Other patents pending

1985 All Rights Reserved

Patent Numbers 4,284,036; 4,491,088 and 4,344,456 • Other Patents Pending

Ziggity Systems

THE SERIES 300 E-Z SIP START-GROW WATERING SYSTEM FOR CAGED BIRDS OF ANY AGE

THE SERIES 800 VERTICAL CUP SYSTEM

For those who prefer cups, the Ziggity Series 800 is an alternate installation in the Start-Grow Watering System. For starting day-old birds, the wire partition slot needs to be two inches lower. When used with a float ball, the cups are self-filling. The Series 800 has the same E-Z Sip Drinker, uses the same regulator and the same water pressure.

Featuring the E-Z Sip Drinker with exclusive triple seat seal.

This system features:
- A totally enclosed sanitary watering system.
- Starts day old birds in cages.
- Adjusts easily for bird growth.
- 360° side to side action drinker makes drinking easy.
- Ziggity Flo Regulator operates efficiently on less than ½ lb. pressure.

- Drinkers attach to start-grow units with easy snap-on feature.
- Drinkers are self-cleaning.
- Available with one or two drinkers on each side of the partition.
- Drinkers have triple seat seal to prevent leakage.
- Plastic pipes never corrode and are virtually trouble-free.

ZIGGITY Z SYSTEMS INC.

Ziggity Systems, Inc.
P.O. Box 1169
Middlebury, IN 46540
219-825-5849

Promotional material for the Series 300 E-Z Sip Start-Grow watering system for caged birds of any age.

required doing something that was adjustable in height location because of bird growth. That required slotting the cage partition which was 1″ X 1″ wire three inches from the bottom to almost the top one-inch wide. Two plastic strips were used on each side of the vertical one inch wide, eleven inch high slot. The start-grow unit had two locations for drinkers, one on each side of the partition. It also had a hose barb on it for attaching a rubber hose one-fourth inch I.D. The water supply line was placed on top of the cage that also had a

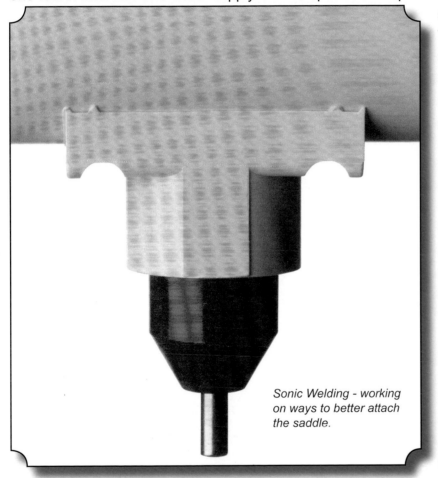

Sonic Welding - working on ways to better attach the saddle.

saddle with hose barb. The rubber hose would act as a means to make connections to supply water. The start-grow was supplied with an eighteen inch long rope that had a hook on the end used for raising the unit as the birds grew. We started looking at the possibility of welding our saddles onto the pipe instead of gluing them.

Several of the working girls got medical problems from the glue fumes. Many changes in saddle design were required to get that to work consistently. The Sonic Welder Manufacturer Company was good at giving advice for trying different things, but the process was a hit and miss system. To get a setup that truly worked every day was very hard to come up with. It took a whole year to do it with many changes on saddle design before it worked properly. The energy directors on each part had to be perfect in order to weld the same. In doing that, I lost much of my hearing because of the high pitch scream that the welding emitted when things weren't correct. Today, we wouldn't think of trying to glue saddles.

In 1984, we were the only company marketing a nipple type drinker for the broiler industry. We were starting to get patents issued on the regulator and drinkers, so we had almost total control over sales in a product. Others copied our product, selling it and using

Start Grow System

Benefits of the Ziggity Start Grow System

"Y" Bracket

- ◆ Birds Start Easier
- ◆ Locates Drinker Away from Side for Easy Access
- ◆ Brackets Adjust Easily with a Special Designed Edge Guard
- ◆ Vinyl Tube Retainer Secures Vinyl Hose
- ◆ Hose Inlet Helps Eliminate Air Locks

Lift System

- ◆ Saves Labor
- ◆ Maintains Perfect Drinker Height
- ◆ Easy Access Winch
- ◆ Conduit System Reduces Drag
- ◆ Adjust Up to 4 Drop Through Levels

The new Ziggity Start Grow System allows for better system management throughout each flock. The "Y" Bracket design allows drinkers to be raised to the top of every cage. This prevents larger birds from accidental triggering of the drinkers. The "Y" Bracket incorporates twin lock drinkers which ensure more secure fastening and better light penetration to the stainless trigger pin. The 360° easy activating drinker has been designed to allow higher column water pressure without increasing the force required to activate the drinker: End result - better chick starts!

All systems incorporate the patented Flush Through Regulators and Flow Through End assemblies for easier maintenance. The optional lift system can be installed to reduce management time and maintain the perfect drinker height.

Promotional material outlining the advantages of the Start Grow System.

all of our efforts; they felt they did not need to pay attention to patents. The company that did that wasn't going to honor any patents or pay any royalties. Our president said the practice had to stop, and our attorney started court action to do so. That became a nightmare for me because the total product design was mine. When depositions started, I had to come up with details on how, why, and when on the total system. That required almost all of my time with both sets of lawyers. It involved two years of gathering information and lawyer delays before actual court action started.

During that period, the president of Ziggity Systems, Lloyd Bontrager, went to Florida with his airplane during spring break with his youngest son. Upon return, they ran into bad weather that forced the plane down, and neither survived. Wilbur was then replaced as president of Ziggity Systems, Inc. in 1985. Larry Schrock stayed on as general manager for a period. Meanwhile, the patent court action kept moving forward slowly.

Turkey growers had tried to use our system with little success on birds over three weeks of age. When they got older, they would attack the trigger pin with force, spilling water all over, and causing wet floors. We stopped selling to turkey growers at that point. The duck growers were having good success starting and growing ducks with our system. Two of the largest duck growing operations in the United Sates are in our backyard. At that point, we had over thirty persons, mostly women, doing home assembly of drinkers. They

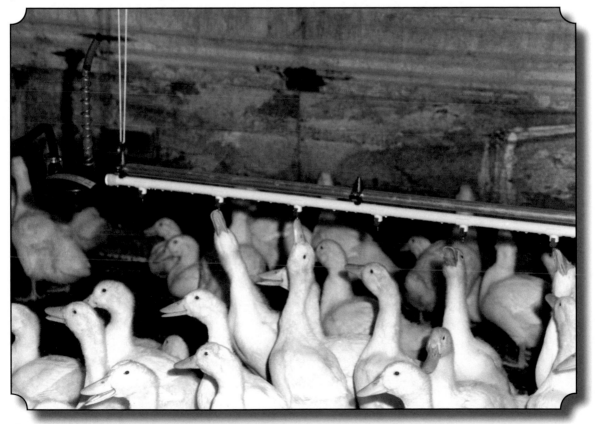

Duck growers had very good success with the nipple type drinker systems.

averaged 6,000 drinkers a week besides the ones our factory workers did. To cut costs on plastic parts, we made new tooling and went to sixteen cavities to start with. We made the electro-guard bracket higher on the floor system at that time.

Hart Cup Manufacturing Company went bankrupt at that point, and no repair parts were available. We made a change in our drinker so it could be converted into a cup type that would work as a replacement for Hart cup parts. We sold many thousands of those for several years. After several years, the bankruptcy was settled, and the tooling was sold to people who were going to make Hart cup parts available again. We stopped trying to sell cups and worked on trying to convert most of them to nipple type drinkers.

The color of the natural A.B.S. material was an off-yellow that allowed some sunlight to penetrate. In southern exposure to sunlight, algae started to grow inside the pipe. It cost considerably more to color it white but, when asked, most distributors wanted white. We changed to white on the pipe and all parts that went with it. We designed a low pressure plastic gate valve to be used on the far end of water lines, also, for all other places where a full flow valve was needed.

In 1986, we moved to 12663 U.S. 20 East to a larger building with a loading dock and six offices.

A view of the next facilities Ziggity Systems, Inc. moved into in 1986.

Poultry men started to use chlorine to clean waterlines. When they used a stronger solution, it affected our seat in the drinker. When we tested for failure, we needed a stronger mixture in order to clean the inside of the pipe. It was necessary to find still another kind of seat material that chlorine would not damage. We started with P.V.C. material, and it failed because of plastizer incompatibilities. We changed to Kraton material, but it failed due to molding knit line problems. The E.P.D.M. worked if no more than the normal part mixture of chlorine was used than that allowed by a municipality. It was brought to our attention that a product called C-Flex was being used by hospitals to put into humans and animals. Those tubes and parts were being made in Florida. We asked for samples to test in different chlorine mixtures. The C-Flex material was placed in chlorine mixtures, 1/3 strength, 2/3, and full strength, leaving them sit for three weeks with E.P.D.M. with them. The E.P.D.M. was severely damaged, and the C-Flex didn't show any damage. Jeff Yoder, our Quality Control Manager, and I started planning to get a single cavity mold made that would make a seat with no knit line. Bender Mold and Machine was asked to do that. It was shipped to Concept Polymers, Inc. Clearwater, Florida, for sample parts. They made samples of C-Flex seats for us to try. The sample parts didn't seat, the C-Flex seat was too hard. It was checked and found to be over seventy durometers; the E.P.D.M. seats were fifty durometers. They assured us that they could soften the material to fifty durometers by adding Plasticizers to the formula to soften it. Why didn't we remember that Plasticizer added to anything is a "No, no" on A.B.S. material? We got sample seats that were softened to fifty durometers; they seated well and were tested to see if the Plasticizer had done a change on chlorine. We found that it had not. We went to Bender Mold and Machine and ordered a sixteen cavity mold, made special with no knit lines. When completed it, was shipped to Concept Polymers to make seats.

We had millions of those in use when reports started to come in that the ball was sticking to the seat. Birds weren't able to get any water in cages, and that became a big problem. We got the E.P.D.M. seat back into production to help customers; we had to warn them not to use chlorine to clean water lines. We later had the same problem with plastic hose on start-grow units. The barbs would fall off the saddle on start-grow units due to Plasticizer in the hose. We found a company that could make soft P.V.C. hose without a Plasticizer that was reactive to A.B.S. material. That was our biggest failures involving A.B.S. material.

Start-up cup that was designed to help start de-beaked chicks.

All of that was happening during our depositions period by patent lawyers. Some integrators asked us to provide a day-old start-up cup to attach to a drinker location that was self-filling to help start de-beaked birds. We met the challenge and provided one that snapped on the pipe at day one and then was removed in about fourteen days. It was self-filling with a spring under it that shut the water off when the water weight in the cup depressed the spring. The assembly dropped away from the trigger pin when full, then added water as birds consumed it.

We started to get reports of excess water flow in our year old drinkers with some pressure settings that caused a wet floor. We had drinkers returned for inspection and found the eyelet had worn a total of one thousandth in diameter, and that allowed twice

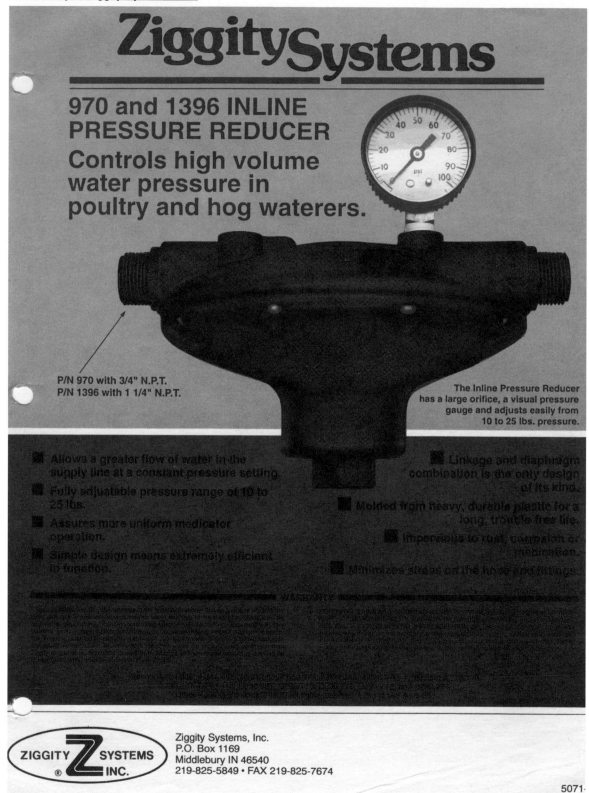

A Ziggity Systems flyer explaining the details of the 970 and 1396 inline pressure reducer.

as much water to flow at the same pressure setting. That proved that some water will have an effect on eyelet wear, and soon more of those kinds of reports came in. The difference of hole diameter of the eyelet and the diameter of the trigger pin are called clearance. When the hole wears, that allows more water to flow when triggered. We overcame that problem by inserting a metering pin in the cap hole. It rested on the ball; when activated, it controlled the flow rate. When birds triggered the pin, the ball moved up, so did the metering pin, but there never was any pressure to wear that part. It was also made of plastic that didn't float. Thus was born a totally new way to control flow rate in a nipple drinker. We then added a two-stage one that had two different diameters that were located in the cap hole. When triggered side to side, the larger diameter worked up and down in the cap hole. When lifted by older birds, the smaller diameter on the pin went into effect, allowing much more water flow with the same pressure setting. That feature sold many drinkers. We had a ten pound regulator available to be used on water supply lines.

The industry wanted a higher pressure range regulator to control water supply lines. On large well pumps operating on start-stop pumping, the line pressure would vary by twenty pounds or more. That change would also affect the regulator on the water lines. We then introduced our high pressure inline regulator that adjusted from ten to twenty-five pounds. Hog producers used it on their nipple type drinkers. What this did was keep the pressure constant at one pressure setting to the nipple drinkers. That helped keep floors dry for hogs and chickens when they activated the trigger pin for a drink.

In the fall of 1988, we moved to the new plant located at 101 Industrial Parkway, Middlebury, Indiana. We were the first to move into the new Industrial Park. The town failed to have city water to our location; we had to install a well in order to have water.

The new Ziggity Systems, Inc. manufacturing plant, fall of 1988.

In 1989, Larry Schrock left as general manager to spend full time at a cheese house operation he had interest in. L & W Engineering hired Brad Donahoe to take his place as general manager of Ziggity Systems, Inc. Many cage operators were still using Hart cups in cage layers, so a need developed for a start-grow cage cup drinker that would fit into our start-grow nipple units. We designed and tooled one to work with the start-grow attachments. That made it possible to place a cup and nipple type drinker in alternate partitions in each cage partition. That, then, made it possible for all birds in a start-grow house to know how to drink from both cup and nipple types in each cage. Bird loss in layer

Big "Z"
2.5" Turkey Poult System

Benefits of the 2.5" Turkey Poult System

◆ Improves Performance

◆ Better Feed Conversion

◆ Reduced Disease Problems

◆ Lower Medication Costs

◆ Labor Savings

◆ Dryer Floors

◆ Lower Cost for Shavings

◆ No Drinkers to Wash

◆ Lower Maintenance Cost

◆ Recommended for Birds up to 6 Weeks

Ziggity Systems introduces a 2.5" Big "Z" drinker for turkey poults. Years of testing have shown turkeys need a larger drinker in order to thrive.

They also need to see the water in order to consume the amount required for proper growth. Because turkeys tend to attack a trigger pin drinker at several weeks of age, Ziggity has developed a specially designed drinker so they can see water and adjust to proper drinking habits. Ziggity's exclusive system results in good weight gains and the desired water intake. Field testing has proven the 2.5" drinker is the wave of the future for turkey poults. Growers who use this drinker comment on its ability to stay clean which results in reduced labor, lower medication costs and producing a better end product.

Ziggity helps grow a good turkey!

Big "Z" Turkey Poult System flyer used to show the benefits of using this system for Turkeys.

cages could be a big economic factor if the started pullets came from a start-grow house that had a different kind of drinker. That sometimes led to a high percentage of adult bird loss the first week. All start grow cages have wire floors that allow all bird waste to drop down onto the lower birds. Those levels can be as many as four high. We had to make an umbrella-like cover to keep the overhead waste from falling into the cup. The top level didn't need the covers. After several years, all layer houses were changed over to nipple type drinkers; we have no market today for any cup systems.

We made a one-inch diameter black pipe system for adult turkey drinkers. That required a bigger saddle, bigger diameter drinker with a five-eighth inch diameter ball and a much larger diameter trigger pin. A line of that system was placed in a turkey house of adult birds in Minnesota. It took several days for them to learn to drink from the trigger pins. After they learned, they did the same thing they had done with our standard system. They hit the trigger pins with their large beaks and spilled water everywhere. The line was removed before a total grow out was done. We then stopped selling any of the standard systems to turkey growers. We needed to do some research closer to Ziggity Systems to find what was needed to make turkeys stop attacking the trigger pin. We made an open shield that welded onto the end of the drinker body. It was to prevent laying hens from inadvertently triggering the drinkers with their bodies because of the low profile cages.

We designed and applied for patents on an automatic flushing setup on the watering system. We had found that growers who frequently flushed the water lines had fewer leakage problems. However, that was a task that took a lot of time. It meant having workers located at both ends of water lines to open and shut valves when flushing lines. We made a self-sealing stand pipe cap for the regulator stand pipe and also for the end assembly. We also made a new end assembly that opened with 2½ pounds of water pressure. We made a manual bypass startup at the regulators that required turning on a plastic gate valve which pressured the water lines to full pressure flush. That removed all sediments that had formed in the low pressure water lines. The automatic spring loaded end assembly was connected to the outside with a hose line. That required only turning the valve at the regulators to flush the lines. It took one minute per 100 feet of line to complete the flush. It was soon requested that we also make that automatic with a clock. We made a special part on the system that made it possible. Included was a lawn sprinkler clock that had different zone controls. Each zone control would handle a fixed number of regulators which was determined by size of water supply line. The automatic valve used is the same type used on dishwashers. Most all cage operators already used the system, and that helped keep all lines free of sediment. Low water pressure in the lines allows sediments to form. Some broiler growers have also seen the merits of frequent line flushing.

The attorneys finally had all documents ready to go to court. We left by airplane with fifteen boxes full of papers. The boxes were like those used to store year-end records, and

Electronic Solenoid Flush System

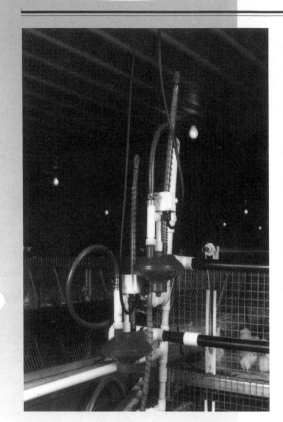

Ziggity Electronic Solenoid Flush System is designed for maximizing bird performance and longevity of your Ziggity System. The Solenoid Flush Unit easily adapts to all Ziggity Flush Through Regulators. When combined with the Automatic Flush Ends and the 12 Station Control Clock, every line can be programmed for automatic flushing.

The Control Clock allows three programmable flush cycles every day. Each unit can control up to 12 regulators for independent flushing or 24 regulators for semi-independent flushing, the flush cycle can be set for as little as 1 minute.

The Electronic Flush System is used to remove air locks and sediment. Air locks form during the night while birds are not consuming water. All water has some level of dissolved oxygen; as water warms up it causes oxygen to separate out thus contributing to air locks. These air locks can be removed automatically with the solenoid flush system.

If your farm includes Broilers, Breeders, Layers, Pullets or Turkeys the Automatic Solenoid Flush System is your solution to improving performance and simplifying maintenance of your nipple drinking system.

Ziggity helps grow a good chicken!

Benefits of the Ziggity Electronic Flush System

◆ Supplies Cool Fresh Water Instantly

◆ Reduces Air Locks

◆ Keeps Drinker Lines Clean

◆ Helps Increase Water Consumption

◆ Simplifies Management

◆ Contributes To Increased Bird Efficiency

◆ Fully Automatic

A flyer explains the benefits of the Ziggity Systems, Inc. electronic solenoid flush system.

U.P.S. brought us about the same amount two days later. That completed the information required for the judge. We were in court in front of the judge for two weeks; at that time, no one seemed to be enjoying themselves except the attorneys. We heard nothing from the judge for many months. Cost on that kind of involvement went way beyond reason. We continued work at Ziggity trying to improve our drinkers. It was hard to concentrate when wondering what was taking the judge so long to make a decision. We had competition introducing new systems that were taking away some sales at that time. We needed to look at ways that could help the installation crews cut down on time required to install the nuts and bolts on our system. Some imported systems had the drinkers already installed on the pipes, along with the support channel. In 1991, we heard from the judge that he ruled our patent was valid, and that he ruled in our favor on our damages. That amounted to a considerable amount of money. There were several meetings between our attorneys and the defendant's attorneys before a complete deal was made. The pressure regulator patent became an issue before it all was settled; they paid a fixed amount on sales already completed. L & W Engineering asked if Dale and I would consider acquiring their fifty-two percent at the May 31, 1991, year end meeting. They determined what they thought the fifty-two percent would be worth. They ended up with the funds from the legal court case plus the loan we had to make to cover the rest. Starting a new year in June 1991, Dale and I owned Ziggity Systems, Inc. In one year, we paid off our loan.

In 1992, we decided to make a stamped stainless steel seat to help overcome the problems we had with E.P.D.M. seats getting damaged by chlorine. That required many changes in the drinker bodies and caps. Twin Lock and Single Lock drinker bodies had to be changed to get it done. After we had the changeover completed, we also had the Big Ace Drinker changed to a ½" diameter ball and stamped stainless steel seat. That also required a new cap that held the seat. On the changeover in the Twin Lock to Single Lock and Big Ace Drinker, the cap became the flow control unit. The cap held the seat, the ball rested on the seat, the metering pin rested on the ball, and the top of the cap was the o-ring. That type assembly was called capsule unit. It made it easy to change flow rates on drinkers. Different hole diameters in cap and metering pin diameters changed flow rates. The export market wanted a system made up with lock-together parts that fit our pipe. They would then have a local company make pipe to our size pipe and buy all of the lock-on parts from us to complete a system. We did that and sold many parts that went to Brazil and the Far East. However, those parts were copied when usage numbers made it profitable.

It was found that turkeys quit hitting the trigger pin if a small diameter disc was located on the end of it. Water would collect on it and when they could see water and placed their beaks next to it, the water would flow into their mouths. We started putting a small stainless disc on every drinker for turkeys. We received a letter from Chore-Time telling us

Big Z Turkey System

Benefits of the Ziggity Big Z Activator for Turkeys

- ◆ Improves Bird Performance

- ◆ Improves Feed Conversion

- ◆ Reduces Disease Problems

- ◆ Lower Medication Costs

- ◆ Reduces Labor Costs

- ◆ Dryer Floors

- ◆ Lower Cost for Shavings

- ◆ No Drinkers to Wash

- ◆ Lower Maintenance Cost

Ziggity Systems introduces a Big Z Activator for turkey poults. Years of testing have shown turkeys need a larger drinker in order to thrive.

They also need to see the water in order to consume the amount required for proper growth. Because turkeys tend to attack a trigger pin drinker at several weeks of age, Ziggity has developed a specially designed drinker so they can see water and adjust to proper drinking habits. Ziggity's exclusive system results in good weight gains and the desired water intake. Field testing has proven the Activator System is the wave of the future for turkey production. Growers who use this Activator comment on its ability to stay clean which results in reduced labor, lower medication costs and producing a better end product.

Ziggity helps grow a good turkey!

A flyer explains the benefits of the Ziggity Systems, Inc. Big Z Turkey System.

they had a patent on that design. As the turkeys grew, so did their beaks. We noticed that a bigger diameter retainer would be better. So, we made one 2½" in diameter in silver color and tried it. It worked better, so I signed an agreement with Chore-Time that we wouldn't sell any disc type under 2½" in diameter. Patents showed many cups had expired long ago in that size range.

We soon found that silver wasn't the best color for turkeys. A turkey grower in southern Indiana called and shared something about color's effect on turkey eye sight. He had gone to a local ice cream stand that sold soft ice cream. They had many different things to sprinkle over the ice cream. One was many different colored chips. He got a small amount of those and put them on the feed for day-old turkeys to see whether that would help them start eating feed. To his surprise, they flocked on the pans where he placed them. However, upon close observation, he saw they were only eating the green ones. When he reported that to Brad Donahoe, we got into the car and went to his farm in southern Indiana to check his findings. Turkeys, as a rule, are quite dumb. If you set an empty bucket into a pen of turkeys and walk away, you'll find upon your return that it will be full of dead turkeys. One will hop into the bucket and start to scream, and the rest will follow until the bucket is full.

We took off one 2½" diameter silver disc and painted it John Deere green and went to lunch to let it dry. Upon return, we placed the green unit back into a pen of several hundred turkeys. What happened after that is beyond words to describe. The birds started to pile on each other to get next to the green disc. That forced the ones next to it under the disc, and water started to spill on them. We couldn't push them back because they were all coming toward us. When a loud noise happens, they run for cover. We clapped to stop them and quickly removed the green disc. We returned home to the office and ordered enough green discs to change the whole house. That got all turkeys started on water much quicker. Today, all turkey watering sold is green and it's easy to understand why that color works best. We started recommending only our 2½" diameter disc on bird usage up to six weeks. We now have a 4" diameter disc that is being used on female turkeys up to market age. Tom turkeys are still a challenge to get to market age. At the start, we had been welding a wrap-adapter bottom on every floor system pipe; five of those were placed two feet apart. The other half of the wrap-adapter was called the top; the top hooked onto the bottom and was fastened with a bolt around the galvanized support pipe.

Some installation crews complained about all the bolt work on our support system. We designed a one piece snap-on around both pipes that could work as support for anti-roost wire and overhead support. That part snapped together and was much quicker to install. It needed to be placed at a welded saddle in order to keep pipe from rotating.

My son, Robert, married Angelika Jende from Hamburg, Germany, and they made plans to move back to the United States and join Ziggity Systems in foreign sales work. His

Slope Neutralizer

Benefits of the Ziggity Slope Neutralizer

◆ Designed for Drinker Lines Which Exceed 4" or 10cm of Fall

◆ Automatically Adjusts to Regulator Pressure

◆ Reduces Water Pressure Without Water Restriction

◆ Simplifies Management

◆ Eliminates Water Pressure Increase During Low Consumption Periods

◆ Allows High Pressure Flush With Minimal Back Pressure

◆ Exclusive Design Without Springs or Gaskets

◆ Easy Installation on Floor or Cage Systems

◆ Maintenance Free

Ziggity Systems, Inc. • 101 Industrial Parkway
P.O. Box 1169 • Middlebury, Indiana 46540-1169 • U.S.A
Office +1 219-825-5849 • Fax +1 219-825-7674

5109-98

The advantages of the Slope Neutralizer are explained in some Ziggity Systems, Inc. marketing material.

production setup, managed by Geoff Taylor, was moved from Holland to England - Avtron UK, Lower Nill, Hook Norton, Banbury, Oxfordshire, United Kingdom. Keith Gladfelter was domestic sales manager in the United States. Ziggity stock was transferred from my shares to Robert to cover his assets.

In 1995, we weren't consistently getting quality stainless steel seats from our suppliers. That was affecting the performance in the field on our drinkers. The salesperson in the field assured us something had to be done to get our drinker seat to work better. At our summer sales meeting and company picnic, they all voted to get a good quality machined seat made. We had been checking with many companies on machined seat cost made by Swiss Machines. Those machines are slow, and that made costs go up. We found a company in New York State that would make a seat and eyelet combination, but it wouldn't coin the part on the Swiss Machine. Next, we made plans to have a custom-made machine that would do the coining automatically. We ordered that machine with a six month delivery date. When delivered, it wouldn't coin the seats to specifications. The machine was returned for change on coining cylinders, and that took several more months. We started to receive our order of two million machined seats from New York State, but had no machine that could coin them. When the reworked machine came back, it was a little better, but failed to duplicate coining to specifications required.

In 1996, nothing was working on the machine seat project; I called the stamped seat supplier and asked whether he would consider trying .035 stainless steel on a 9/32" diameter ball seat. They asked for a print on the design which we faxed to them. They gave us a quote, and we waited several months for parts to test. We also had to have a new trigger pin made. I still had in my mind a totally new system that would help in all areas of improving a watering system. The pipe would be P.V.C. to help resist chemicals. It would be made with the same I.D. as the one inch black pipe. It had two parallel strips five-eighths inch apart running the full length of the 10' pipe. Those strips would hold the drinker in place at any location where a hole was made between the two strips. The P.V.C. had to be drilled because the material would crack when punched. I had 2,500 ten-foot pipes made to install for test purposes in many locations in the states. I hand-coined 25,000 machined parts on a steel block with a small hammer. I did that work above the engineering room in the back of Ziggity. When I had enough parts to do a house, I would take off and help install it. Stan Lowery in Watkinsville, Georgia, got the first house, and it's still in use with the first set of drinkers. He has had to replace less than ten drinkers in nine years of usage.

We started to get parts for 9/32" diameter balls and seats, and trigger pins. The first tests showed that they were a big improvement. Making the ball smaller required a smaller diameter hole in the seat, thus cutting down in seating area, so it made for better seating. Because of less weight, it also triggered more easily for baby chicks when adjusted to low line pressure. The stainless steel seat supplier was instructed to get a very precision punch made to coin the seat area and to run only a certain number of parts before replacing the punch.

In 1997, we went to the International Poultry Show, and I instructed all the salesmen on the changeover made in the drinker. I told them not to tell customers about it because it hadn't been field tested yet. Salesmen's spirits were at a low level; we had failed in getting the machined seat into production because of the coining failure, and they had lost confidence in a stamped seat. The rubber seat worked great if they could keep operators from running high levels of chlorine in the system. I was confident the new 9/32″ diameter unit would work much better. I didn't want to tell the industry before we had field testing results. Ziggity Systems didn't want another replacement program like we had with the C-Flex seat problem. In order to accomplish the changeover, I personally paid for it. During discussion on doing that, it was clear that no one had confidence in it. Therefore, I chose to do it on my own because doing nothing wasn't good, either.

It was two years before we started to tell the public about the merits of the small ball system. It since has been proven to have been one of the better improvements of our system. We then tried to make the seat for the Big Ace turkey and breeder hen drinker with a smaller seven-sixteenth inch ball and seat. That helped, but the seat area was still larger than on the five-sixteenth inch diameter broiler seat. The seat supplier couldn't get a seat consistent in quality. On the stamped seat, we found high spots in the coining areas where we could see that the material had hard elements in it. When the seat was placed under two hundred magnifications, several high spots could be seen that didn't form to the punch. The ball then rested on them and that allowed leakage.

We found a supplier that could machine a seat that met the qualities that were needed for a better seat.

The sales in Big Ace drinkers increased because of the improved machined seat for turkeys and breeder hens. We had an air-operated seat tester made to check seat quality. We scrapped the two million stainless seats after it was determined that the coining machine couldn't be made to work. We made a new start-grow V-bracket out of Polypropylene, a one piece unit with two elbows, one on each arm. It had a hose barb on it, also. That unit was made to straddle the support bars in the top of cage partitions. With that unit, it was possible to raise the drinkers to the top of the cage so birds wouldn't hit drinkers with their bodies.

In 1998, we introduced a newly designed slope neutralizer that adjusted automatically to line pressure from the regulator adjustment; that was done without springs. Water was directed into a small chamber that had two 7/16″ diameter seats installed at the two inlets with balls seated on them. A small washer weight was added to get four inch and six inch differentials. The chamber had a removal lid with a stand pipe attachment and self-sealing cap. The chamber was made with an outlet for one inch pipe; it also had a reducer plug for adapting to the three-fourths inch diameter pipe. At our annual yearly sales meeting, many integrators were asking the salesmen for twenty-four inch length stand pipes on our systems. I knew that if we provided them, wet floor problems would increase. I have learned much from actual farm contact experience in my life in traveling with poultry persons. When a pipe is supplied that makes it possible to run water pressure at almost one pound, customers will use it, not considering that it might be the cause of wet floor problem. We had done that and got our big problem with wet floors. We started with twelve inch stand pipes and had less wet floors.

In 1999, we made a new type of lift system for start-grow pullet cage systems, a system that lifted all start-grow units together at the turn of a gear reducer. A twenty to one gear reducer was placed on top of the cage row on one side over start-grow units. In a 400 foot cage row, the gear reducer would be located at a 200 foot location. The pipe was supported by riser stands at each partition. All levels of start-grow units are interconnected to the top unit, which has a rope on it. The top level rope was fastened with some tension to the one-half inch diameter conduit pipe. When the gear head was turned, all start-grow units lifted together, and that was a great labor saver. Before that gear head unit, all start-grow units had to be adjusted individually with a rope having a hook on the end.

Lift System
Simplify flock management and reduce the worry that each bracket is adjusted to the proper height. The Lift System allows up to 4 drop through levels to be connected and adjusted with one winch. The conduit roll over design reduces tension buildup by lifting the cord vertically. Thus eliminating bracket bind which is common in competitive type winch systems. Each line is controlled with a rachet type locking winch.
Save Time, Money and labor with Ziggity's Start Grow System.

Due to the design of the saddles, we had to use A.B.S. material. That is Acrylonitrile-Butadiene-Styrene and is the only material that welds with a sonic electronic plastic welder. When we went to bigger diameter pipe for turkey tests, we used one inch pipe size so that all plastic pipe fittings would work. That also made it possible to weld the bigger saddles onto the pipe. That pipe was later used on the Big Ace Twin Lock broiler system for the longer broiler house buildings and cage houses. The cost of the white three-fourth inch pipe kept increasing because of material costs. We had to change the pipe color from white to black in order to make the small pipe competitive in the market place. We were surprised that many distributors didn't want to accept the change. We did make a few orders of white pipe at increased costs before they all changed over because of the high cost of white A.B.S. material. Today, all distributors use the three-fourth inch diameter black with no problem. Change isn't easy to accept by some distributors.

In 2000, most all engineering efforts were diverted to get all old prints onto the computer. Many had to be updated; we didn't try for any new products until that task was completed. I had turned management of the operation over to Dale and Robert at that point. I told my family I was going to sell my interest in Ziggity Systems, Inc. when the Hudson Car Museum was completed in Shipshewana, Indiana.

I did install some test drinkers at some locations for observation. I worked with Dick Bender at Bender Mold at trying to get closer tolerances on individual cavities to each other. We had a problem keeping all parts within close tolerance. If molds had over thirty cavities, close tolerance was a requirement when working with water flow. A few tenths of a thousand difference can cause all kinds of problems in flow control. How we ever got as far as we have without all the test equipment we have now has to be called a miracle! The key to performance on watering equipment for poultry is all of the before mentioned, plus the use of the right plastic material for the parts. Design of the cavity and gate for material flow has a great effect on parts. We made our share of unwanted mistakes, but we tried to take care of them with improvements.

My father taught me this, "A quitter never wins and a winner never quits." That motto has kept me involved in this kind of work. I have had an interesting life trying to make poultrymen's work easier and more profitable. The thing that got me started in this direction was the first job away from home at Creighton Brothers, Warsaw, Indiana. I saw a need for automatic feeders and waters. Concern for that need has been a total effort on my part, as well as with the start of the E-Z Feeder that was sold to Buckeye Incubator Company, Springfield, Ohio. I also had twenty years of feeding and watering experiences while working with Chore-Time.

My last years were spent with Ziggity Systems, Inc., Middlebury, Indiana on closed watering systems.

Chapter 14

Start of the Hudson Motor Car Company

In 1906, Roy D. Chapin was a salesman for Oldsmobile; he also had ambitions to become an owner of a car company. He met with the owner of Thomas Flyer Car Company, a man with cash reserves who made only high priced big cars that sold well. Mr. Chapin sold the man on the merits of having a lower priced car to sell with his present high priced models. After several days of discussion and games of golf, an agreement was made to have a cheaper model car introduced by Thomas Flyer. A new company was formed to manufacture the new car. E.R. Thomas was the President; Roy D. Chapin was General Manager; Fred Bezner was Secretary; Howard Coffin was Vice President; and James Brady was Second Vice President. Every board member put money into the corporation. The new corporation was called Thomas-Detroit. The car was called Thomas Flyer No. 40. Roy had promised to make and deliver 500 cars in a year. By June 1907, the 500 cars had been delivered. They made a good profit on that venture. During the second year, they made 750 cars. The men responsible for the success of the second year began to think of themselves as real manufacturers of cars. The parent company (Thomas-Buffalo) controlled the number of cars that were sold. Thomas-Detroit had no control over sales: they only made low-priced cars.

Roy D. Chapin had visions of being in control of sales, but breaking with Thomas-Detroit was out of the question, Roy was only twenty-eight years old. Hugh Chalmers, a good super sales person that made a $72,000 annual salary, had resigned from the National Cash Register Company. Roy contacted the man and encouraged him to buy all of Mr. Thomas's car stock. Chalmers purchased controlling interest in Thomas-Detroit in the fall of 1908. They changed the name of the company to Chalmers-Detroit Motor Company. They started with two models in the 1909 model year. The cheaper model, the "30," sold for $1,500, and the No. 40 Roadster sold for $2,750. After several months, it was established that those models weren't selling as well as they had planned, and R.B. Jackson, Roy's friend, came on the scene. He left Olds and had plans to make a four cylinder car for less than $1,000. That design was made into what was called a Model 20 Car. They found that it could be made to sell for less than a thousand dollars. They decided to break away from the Chalmers-Detroit Motor Car Company and establish their own sales program. For that, they needed cash to advertise and set up dealerships. R.B. Jackson had married the niece of J.L. Hudson, who owned Detroit's Hudson Department Store. Mr. Jackson asked Mr. Hudson if he would consider investing in a new car company. After some consideration, he decided to help the three owners on the new adventure, loaning them $90,000. In response, they named the cars after him. They had their first Hudson Motor Car Company meeting of record on March 6, 1909. The advertisement emblem triangle that overlaid all Hudson ads symbolized the partnerships of Chapin, Coffin, and Bezner and they agreed to stick together regardless of what might happen. They had many ups and downs the first ten years. However, all three were able to live up to what they had promised each other.

Roy spent time with a government position during World War I. Things became quite disorganized when Roy was president of an organization that was set up to use trucks rather than trains to move troops and material. Hudson Car Company was set up to make military munitions during the war. Roy was faced with procurement problems when the war ended, and that cut into car sales. It was at a time when there was a great need for better roads for automobile traffic. He set himself up to be involved in getting the Lincoln Highway completed across the United Sates. Hudson cars were getting bigger, and Roy saw a need for a much smaller car, so they made one called the Essex. That was done in 1919 and it was a great success. In the first year, sales were over 41,000.

In 1922, Roy decided to make a closed Essex car that cost only one hundred dollars more than an open car. That closed car was an instant success and helped Hudson Motor Car Company get out of debt and make a good profit. They sold 26,000 Hudsons and 35,000 Essex cars in 1922 and made $7,000,000 profit. Soon after that period, Roy resigned as president and took the official title of "CEO of Hudson Motor Car Company." He and his family did some traveling and started to think about a new home. In December of 1925, they purchased seven and a half acres on Lake Shore Road, Grosse Point Farms. John Russell Pope was the architect for the new home. He had made the Georgian styled homes which they wanted for their new home.

In the years 1924 to 1929, Roy was looked upon as one of the important persons in the automotive world. He had vision on the importance of the family, the car for the family, and the need for better roads for family use.

In 1929, sales on Hudson Car Company Cars were more than Chrysler Corp., Inc. sales in dollars and numbers. Hudson sold over 300,000 cars and made over $11,000,000 in profit, the best year in its history. During the next few years, surviving the Depression period took a lot of effort, but they were successful in doing that. In 1932, they changed the name of the Essex car to Terraplane and had Amelia Earhart christen a new 1933 model Roadster. She was a famous aviatrix, and that brought many important figures to the ceremony. Chapin had a great gift for salesmanship and made the event noteworthy all over the United States. It went down as a historical event in the automobile industry. Hudson used the Terraplane name for the low priced car from 1933 to the end of 1938.

In 1929, Roy was asked to serve in President Hoover's new administration as Secretary of Commerce. Mr. Hoover wanted Mr. Chapin to work with business and industry and help with road building. At first, Roy declined to accept the position because of the problems the depression had on the Hudson Motor Car Company. However, Hoover kept asking for his services. In 1932, in the last period of the Hoover administration, he decided to accept the post of Secretary of Commerce. That was when the depression was the most severe. The public had elected Theodore Roosevelt in November 1932; he took office March 4, 1933. One of the first things the Roosevelt presidency did was to close all banks and made rules on the way they could reopen under the Federal Deposit Insurance Company or F.D.I.C. Rules. That caused a business crisis with all banks closed and not allowed to open until they had required funds in escrow. Think about what would happen today if all banks had to shut their doors until personnel from the government told them whether they qualified to open for business. (I remember well when that happened in 1933; the Shipshewana Bank closed for a period because it lacked escrow funds to qualify for F.D.I.C. Insurance.) All business transactions stopped except for using the cash you had on hand. That made an extreme hardship on the Hudson Motor Car Company, which was selling cars by installment. Hudson had lost several million dollars in 1932 because of bank failures and installment selling of new cars that had to be reclaimed. Roy returned to the management of Hudson after Hoover lost his re-election bid. He totally redesigned the 1934 model after he was able to get a $6,000,000 loan. He went on a very intensive advertising program selling Hudson and Terraplane cars. They made over $600,000 profit in 1934 and continued to do well the next several years on that sales program.

In late January of 1936, Roy went to Washington to a highway traffic meeting during which he caught a bad cold. Upon his return to Detroit, he thought a game of indoor tennis might help get rid of it, but doing so made him come down with pneumonia. He felt worse after the game and never recovered. He passed away February 16, 1936; he devoted his whole life to the automobile improvements. He made many firsts: a balanced crankshaft, first closed car under $1,000, fender-mounted spares, adjustable front seats, semi-automatic shifting, and many more small ones. This is a condensed version of Hudson Motor Car history.

Chapter 15

The History of Hudson Cars in My Life

When I was fourteen years old, Ervin Yoder, an Amish neighbor boy, left for Texas. He was going to help in the wheat harvest north into Canada. He was nineteen years old and had helped my father with corn harvest for several years. Dad thought Ervin might not return to help with the next corn harvest. My father farmed 280 acres total: 190 acres belonged to him, and Grandpa Schrock had 90 acres that we farmed for him. Grandpa Schrock was retired, so Dad had all the boys in the area help husk corn in the fall. To our surprise, Ervin returned one evening with a brand new 1936 Hudson Terraplane, (four door sedan, tan colored) equipped with electric hand on the steering post. Ervin helped with the corn harvest and allowed me to learn how to drive the semi-automatic shifting car. That was big time stuff for me; no other car I had ever seen before had that kind of far advanced equipment to offer, and the car was beautiful beyond words. It was four years before I turned eighteen years old, which was the age requirement to get a driver's license. Those were four of the longest years in my life. I had very little money at that point. I was close to my grandfather David Schrock, and I shared with him that I had no plans to join the Amish and wanted a Hudson car. He asked me if I could live up to a sworn vow. If I vowed not to tell anyone, then he would loan me $350 to purchase a 1938 used Hudson in 1940. I kept that vow until after the death of my mother, who passed away in 1998. I purchased the

1938 Hudson in 1940 and drove it two years before I traded it for a 1940, four-door maroon sedan with eight cylinders. I kept that car until the 1948 Step Down model Hudsons were out on display.

My second car, a 1940, four-door maroon sedan with eight cylinders.

After a near fatal accident that caused our daughter to fall out onto the road because the back door opened toward the front, I purchased a new Club Coupe. I drove the 1948 Club Coupe one year and put 100,000 miles on it and then traded for another Club Coupe in 1949. With that Hudson, I pulled a trailer many miles to deliver automatic poultry feeders.

In 1950, I traded the 1949 Club Coupe for a 1950 Commodore, 8-cylinder, four door gold sedan, with all the options that were available. That was the best riding and driving car I ever owned. The Commodore was driven at unreal high speeds. I wore out 180 level Siberling tires that were rated at 60,000 miles in 30,000 miles of driving. I had the 1950 Hudson tuned to top speed of 106 miles per hour. I had a higher compression

My 1950 Hudson, often driven at 100 mph!

head installed and timed to run at high speed. I had a motto, "If I care, thou shall not pass." I had many races on the highway and got chased by cops at times. I never was passed by any cars of the same vintage. I had a small scare of being passed on the Pennsylvania toll road. After driving through the last two tunnels near Carlisle exit, I was cruising at 95 when I looked in my rear view mirror and saw a Nash gaining on me. I thought, "No, a Nash is going to embarrass me." I pressed for all the speed available: however, he kept gaining a little on me when he traveled behind me. When he pulled out to pass, he could get only the front of his Nash to where I sat in my car. The wind off my car kept him from passing me; he fell back and followed me into a gas station. He asked me to open my hood so that he could see what I had done to my car to get it to go so fast. His Nash was equipped with a Nash Healy engine with two carburetors. He said I was the only car he hadn't been able to pass since he got his Nash. I have to wonder who else was looking out for me because I sure wasn't. I don't think there were many sales persons on the road that drove faster than I did during the 50s.

I drove home from Waco, Texas 1,358 miles in twenty-three hours nonstop except for gas and restroom stops. There were no four lane highways out in the country at that time. I had to go right through the center of town in all cities at thirty miles per hour. The only thing that helped back then was that there were no speed limits out on the country roads, so I drove at 100 miles per hour. I kept the 1950 Hudson two years and traded it for a 1952 Twin-H Hudson four door that was faster on take off but had a lower top speed. However, states started to post speed limits on most highways by that time. It was at that time that four lane highway constructions had started, and there were few toll roads then. I kept the 1952 Twin-H Hudson for two years and then traded it for a blue 1954 Twin-H Sedan.

I kept the 1954 Twin-H Sedan for two years and then traded it for a 1956 Chevrolet station wagon. Hudson had merged with Nash, and they became American Motors, Inc. I needed a station wagon, and I traded for the Chevrolet. I wasn't impressed with the small Rambler model. I traded for a Dodge station wagon next.

We drove mostly Dodge cars for several years. We had an Oldsmobile, and a Buick Century diesel car that got very good gas mileage per gallon. The Buick wasn't made for speed and comfort; I drove it for 50,000 miles and traded it for a Chrysler model. We drove mostly Chrysler cars in the later years.

I forgot about Hudsons until after I was married to Esta M. Yoder, who suggested that I needed a hobby to divert some of my energies. Esta had also learned to drive in a Hudson car. So, with both of us being Hudson fans, collecting some of the ones we drove in our youth became interesting.

The first model we purchased was a Hudson Club Coupe, a 1952 model sold by a retiring employee of the Middlebury Post Office. He was moving to Florida upon retirement. That was in 1983, the year that we started buying unrestored and restored Hudsons. It was several years later that we saw a maroon 1937 Hudson Terraplane four door sedan with a for sale sign in a window in Mishawaka near Bender Mold shop. We checked the car out and test drove it. It was a good antique car for the price, so we purchased it. That was the start of our acquiring antique Hudsons and sometimes two antique cars a year for many years. Today, we have over fifty Hudsons of unusual nature and design.

I will list some of what we consider our special one-of-a-kind cars. We have acquired many unusual Hudsons over a twenty year period. When we started, we purchased mostly the ones we were driving: after a while, the older models became very interesting.

Hudson made ten race cars in 1917 and I found one with number one on the engine block. We haven't heard of the existence of another race car; those had a very special type of motor. Hudson started early on to make their own motors.

We have a 1927 Hudson fire truck that wasn't sold by Hudson Motor Car Company. That fire truck was made by a welding shop in Alden, Minnesota. They took a big four door, 1927 Hudson car, removed the body, and made a fire truck on the chassis. It has a 500 gallon per minute pump and 100 gallon water tank to prime the pump.

Many of the old Hudsons needed restorations to make them drivable. We found a 1929 Dover mail truck that was restored by Harrah's collection and sold when he died. Hudson made 500 of those for the government postal department. We have number 425 on our truck.

We found a 1931 seven passenger, 8-cylinder Hudson special built Phaeton. It had no side curtains, the body and instrument panel were 1930, and, from the windshield forward, it was a 1931 car, including the motor and trim. It had two flag pockets on the front and back bumpers. The car had been returned from Panama by a serviceman.

Our 1932, 6-cylinder Essex Sport Roadster was made by Briggs. That car belonged in the Chapin family. The father was president of the Hudson Motor Car Company, and his three sons drove the roadster during their school years.

We found a 1933, 8-cylinder Terraplane that had two side mounts and also a trunk rack and a rumble seat.

We started to print name cards with pictures of four cars on them stating that we collect unusual Hudson cars. We have passed out several thousand of them at car shows. That has given us leads on cars that are for sale.

Here is a list of some of our unusual cars: a 1933 Essex Panel Truck we found in Pennsylvania that was used as a funeral flower car; a 1935 four door, 8-cylinder Hudson equipped with semiautomatic shifting system, two side mounts, wire wheels and fender skirts; a 1936 8-cylinder Hudson, a long wheel base country club four door sedan. That car is also equipped with two side mounts, electric semiautomatic shift, fender skirts, and wig-wag light; a 1936 panel truck that needs to be restored. We purchased a 1937 Terraplane pickup long wheelbase in Texas.

We found a 1937, 8-cylinder Hudson country club sedan in New Hampshire with very low mileage that had been owned by a doctor. It had a serving tray table that adjusted up out of the back of the front seat and also had fender skirts.

We found a 1937 Railton, 8-cylinder on a Hudson chassis made in England and is a right hand drive car.

We also found a 1940 Hudson utility coupe, 6-cylinder car that has a box on rollers that pull out of the trunk for access and use. It's classified as a truck.

Hudson had a policy of selling Hudson chassis to all parts of the world. Therefore, we have an Essex Sport Roadster that was built on a New Zealand body. I know of Hudsons that were built on Australian bodies. Hudson had close ties with the United Kingdom automotive companies. We have two cars with British coach builder bodies on them. Hudson had a custom body builder in Amsbury, Massachusetts, that made car bodies and shipped them by rail to Detroit, Michigan. That was started in 1920 and lasted for ten years; it stopped during the depression.

In the fall of 2004, we went to Tulsa, Oklahoma to a car sale that listed a Murphy Bodied Hudson, 1928 town car. It was the only one ever made. We were prepared to pay whatever price it might take to buy it, and purchased that rare car. The 1928 town car almost completed our collection.

We have many of these rare Hudson restored and show them at prestige invited car shows. The value of old Hudson cars has more than doubled due to this in the last ten years. Young people are now joining the Hudson Club to get leads on Hudsons that are for sale by club members. We have over 3,000 members and they average close to three cars per member. The old original club members bought up all the old cars for parts. They never restored any, just got together, swapped parts, kicked tires, and talked about how to keep Hudsons running.

We took a restored 1951 Hudson Hornet convertible with a cloth top that we painted bright red to an annual meet on a trailer. All of the old members would not speak to us; we were new members. We soon found out what was disappointing them. I was told I was going to make it impossible for older people to get parts at a reasonable price if everybody tried to restore their cars as we had done and just hauled them to car shows. They called my cars "trailer babies."

I have one car that we drive to car shows; it's a 1953 Hollywood coupe with Twin-H-power and is painted red with a white top. It shows up well at local car shows; we never take it for more than 100 miles.

One of my biggest restorations was a 1942 Hudson Woodie Wagon body by Campbell Body Works. All other Woodie Wagons on record as sold by Hudson Motor Car Company in 1942 were made by Cantrell Body Builders. The Hudson Woodie Wagon by Campbell Body Works was found by a bear hunter on top of a mountain just north of Death Valley in California 7,000 feet up. It was used as a trailer and was hooked behind a crawler tractor to bring up supplies and haul what was mined down. The Woodie had no seats, no motor, and no drive train, just four wheels that followed the crawler. It was equipped with extra springs in front and back to handle heavy loads. A Hudson club member went up to check whether it was truly a Hudson Woodie. He found it to be true and reported it in the Hudson publication. A California member checked it out and found the owner was deceased and left everything at the location. The area had become part of a national forest area that couldn't be sold. He opened up the road to the top and removed the Woodie. It was brought to Phoenix, Arizona to a Hudson serviceman. My son lived in Phoenix, so we went to the Hudson service shop to check it out. There sat the Woodie in need of much help. It was suggested that we purchase the Woodie and return it to the original status. The first thing we needed was another Hudson sedan with correct wheelbase. We started looking for a long wheelbase Hudson and, after several months, one was listed in a farm sale in the state of Virginia. My wife had an aunt who lived in Harrisonburg, Virginia. We called her and asked if she could measure the wheelbase on the Hudson sedan, which she did and found it to be the right wheelbase. We called Phoenix and found that the Woodie was still for sale. We then asked the aunt if she could attend the auction and purchase the car. She purchased it for $800, and we brought it back to Indiana. We paid $2,000 for the 1942 Woodie Wagon and had it brought back to Indiana, too. After many years of slow work at Wooden Noga in LaPorte, Indiana, the Woodie was finally done. The total work on the Woodie was completed in ten years and was ready to drive. The Commodore, an 8-cylinder Hudson was used to replace the chassis for the restoration. The only metal used from the original Woodie was the special two rear fenders. All door hinges, handle locks were still usable on the original.

We were invited to bring the Woodie Wagon back to Waterloo, New York where it was made in 1942. Many of the employees that worked for Campbell Body Works spoke about different four-door sedans that were converted to three seat Woodies during the war. That was done mostly on long wheelbase cars which made it possible to haul more passengers. It also qualified the car for a C sticker for more gas per week during WW II. Only one person that had worked for Campbell Body Works remembered doing any Hudson cars. Our Woodie body is all wood with no steel any place on it.

In the late 1920s, Hudson had Murphy Coach Builders in California design cars for them. In 1928 they made several four-door sedans with cloth convertible tops; we have four 1928 Hudson cars with the Murphy Body tags on them.

In 1929, Hudson had their best year in car sales; they were number three ahead of Chrysler Corporation. We have two Hudson models that are in the classic car category, a Club Sedan and Dual-Cowl Phaeton. Those two were made by Biddle and Smart Coach Builders in Amsbury, Massachusetts.

We have a 1929 Essex 6-cylinder Speedabout all aluminum body made by them, also. We know of only one other like it which is at the Reno, Nevada Museum. The Speedabout was one of Mr. Harrah's favorite driving cars. I asked the Reno's museum managers if that car would ever be sold. Her answer was that he asked in his will for that car to be left in the collection, so the answer was "No" in 1997. We kept checking whether anyone had ever heard of another Speedabout. No record of another was in the roster book. Several years later at the Auburn, Indiana auction, one was made available for sale. The Speedabout came out of a museum in Maine; that is one of the many unusual Hudsons in our collection.

Hudson made cars under several names, starting out with Hudson. That was due to the fact that Mr. Hudson from the Hudson Department Store chain loaned them $90,000 to start making cars. The first name added was Essex in 1919 when they entered the low price car competition. They were the first with low priced closed body cars. In 1929, they named all commercial vehicles Dover with a Pegasus winged horse in the center; that was discontinued in 1930. In 1932, the name Essex was dropped and replaced with Terraplane, and Amelia Earhart came to do the honors. The Terraplane name was dropped in 1938; the only name used was Hudson with add ons. There were Pacemaker, Commodore, Hollywood, Twin-H-Power, Hornet, Wasp, and Jet.

Hudson dominated NASCAR racing for three years from 1951 through 1953. That was done due to step-down design with the low body profile and center point steering. Those features provided excellent handling qualities. The 6-cylinder engine equipped with Twin-H-Power with a 308 cubic inch displacement was the driving force of the car. Racing data on record by NASCAR shows how many races were won by Hudson cars after the step down car was introduced. Records show that Hudson won almost all races from 1951 to 1953 by many different drivers of Hudsons. Hudson Motor Car Company was the first automotive company to supply parts to convert race cars to muscle cars for NASCAR racing in the 1950s. The conversion to Twin-H-Power increased the horsepower to 170 H.P. That is why most races were won by those drivers. Some of the first drivers were Marshall Teague, Herb Thomas, Dick Rathmen, Tim Flock, Lou Fegaro, Jim Thompson, Tommy Moon, Jack McGrath, and Frank Mundy.

It has been a mystery to me to hear people who claim to be experts on NASCAR's history when they talk about the early years of racing. They tell about Plymouth and Ford racing on the beach at Daytona Beach, Florida in the late 1940s. Then they skip all of Hudson's complete control of racing in the years of the 50s. Most all of NASCAR and AAA races sponsoring Hudson drivers would finish first, second, third, and sometimes fourth place in a given race. Later in life, when I started to collect and restore Hudsons and was invited to show them at prestige car shows, I was better able to understand why those people didn't want to acknowledge those records. My first such experience was when I took my 1911 Mile-A-Minute Hudson that was totally restored to one of those shows. It was placed in a location with Cadillacs and other cars of the some vintage. The show was judged by three automotive experts in each class. They finished with the Cadillacs after spending at least fifteen minutes going over all points of the car. The person judging the undercarriage was first. He turned and looked at my Hudson from the side and remarked to his companions about the next exhibit, "Looks like we have a Stutz or Marmon Racer next." He walked over to the front of my exhibit and saw the name Hudson on the radiator. He reported back to the other two judges, "It's only a Hudson". Those judges walked around the car, never asked any questions or stopped to look at anything. At that point, I knew it would take time to change people's mind. I have been back to that show with other Hudsons and have found judges that have changed their minds about Hudson cars. It didn't happen only at special invited shows, but at almost any kind of car show. I found that the Hudson name was a negative to many car people. I soon became aware that different people have different opinions about Hudsons, they like them or they hate them to some degree.

We placed many of our best restored Hudsons at the Gilmore Museum in Hickory Corners, Michigan with year models 1909 to 1956, the first year they were made to the last year when a Hudson 308 engine could be bought. It was easier to change opinions when one make of automobile was placed in a room that showed how much Hudson Motor Car Company changed models each year. Some models today are the same for years with almost no changes. We have received many nice letters from many parts of the United States telling us what a special exhibit this is for all to see, and they mention that Hudson redesigned their cars every year in the 30s.

Many people don't know what happened and why no Hudsons were made after 1954. George W. Mason, president of Nash-Kelvinator, called a meeting of the presidents of Hudson, Studebaker, and Packard. The meeting concerned ways the four car companies could survive with the Big Three competition. They decided among themselves that they had to merge. Nash and Hudson merged and called the corporation American Motors, Inc., Studebaker and Packard merged but kept their names. The goal was for each merger to get two good car models introduced to the public that would sell in the next couple of years. Then they would look at another merger to compete with the Big Three auto makers. In the first year of that plan, the president of American Motors. Inc. died suddenly. George Romney was made president of American Motors; Inc., and his goal was to promote only the Rambler. The car market was ready for that kind of car and it sold well. All big car efforts were stopped, and all efforts were placed on Rambler models. When Studebaker and Packard came to talk about merging further, Romney wasn't interest because they had no car model that was selling like the Rambler models. Studebaker and Packard left for Canada and survived a few more years and thus ended the big four plan. American Motors acquired the Jeep that helped to keep American Motors, Inc. going several more years. However, Chrysler Corporation saw that it could be interesting to own the Jeep; thus, another merger or buy out took place. What had been a good plan by the Nash president was then all gone. The most recent car merger was Daimler and Chrysler. There will be more in the near future as the automotive market gets more competitive.

On July 16, 1992 I purchased eight acres of property just south of the Motel 8 in Shipshewana, Indiana. I did that with plans in mind to put my Hudson cars on display to the public. I failed to check what kinds of problems the plan would develop into. Upon checking, I soon became aware of the tax problems it would create. I found out that it only becomes a practical plan when you put a museum under a 501(c)3 status. However, when this is done, the total project — the land, the building, and the cars are community owned and managed by a board. To get the classification wasn't a simple project. I went to Shipshewana and saw the town manager before Christmas of 1997 and asked him if the town already was 501(c)3 status and would be interested in having a car museum. I told my family what I had done at Christmas and why I did it. The town management group came out on February 20, 1998 to see the cars, and they assured us that they would proceed to get that accomplished as soon as possible. Five years after I had purchased the first parcel of land, I was told of another parcel of ten acres that was going to sell next to the first one. We ended up purchasing it; that gave us eighteen acres to build on as one piece of property. It was going to give land to the town for a much bigger financially sound project. The project has taken many turns during the years with improvements made on the project as it moved along.

I had told my two sons that had some interest in Ziggity Systems, Inc. that as soon as the Shipshewana project was completed I would sell my interest in the company, and that they would have first right of refusal on the price, and I signed an agreement to that arrangement.

In the fall of 2004, the project got far enough along that McKibbin Brothers were hired

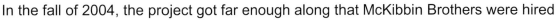

Ground preparation work begins in the fall of 2004 for the construction of a Town Center for Shipshewana. A museum for our Hudsons were included in the plans.

to start work on the site preparation. The town is getting several million dollars toward the project in grants from the state. The enormous amount of paper work involved is also slowing the project.

In order for the project to be self-supporting, the town had to come up with a sound plan. They found a motel builder that was interested in locating a 160 room motel with an adjoining large indoor water park. They would also provide funds to the museum on each room that was rented; that made it possible to get the project going. The motel will manage the museum and exhibition center in conjunction with the town board. The building that will house the cars, the exhibition center, and the visitor bureau will be 200' wide and 250' long. The exhibition center will seat 800 people for banquets and meals. Plans are to make this an attractive place for all car clubs to enjoy and use.

When the project is completed, it will change the Shipshewana area a great deal. The exhibition center can be used for all sorts of activities that fill the needs of the area. Thirty-seven of my cars are going into the museum at first. Those are the only ones we had when the project started.

The time we spent collecting these many unusual Hudsons has been a very rewarding experience for us. We have met so many people that have wanted to share a Hudson story. We have traveled around the world several times in our business work. That has also given us the opportunity to check out Hudson owners in New Zealand and Australia. Many Hudson cars are still being driven in those countries, and some models are quite rare. Many of the cars in our collection are one-of-a-kind types. How did we happen to be at the right place and at the right time to find them? When reflecting, some of our car acquisitions have been most unique, some by incredible means and happenings. We want to give Him the entire honor that made it happen.

Chapter 16

Additional Thoughts and Acknowledgements

I married Edna Yoder during my first year of employment at Creighton Brothers. She was an outstanding woman to put up with my working schedules. We had laying hens in the barn on our rented property which I converted to a laying house. We produced fertile eggs that went to Eli Lilly Labs to make vaccine. Edna took care of these layers when we lived on the Crystal Lake Rental property. We also had to rent boats to those who wanted to fish. I worked most days 10 to 12 hours a day in the hatchery as needed.

The Hostetler family in 1960. Standing (left to right): Ruby Arlene, LeAnna, and Mary Etta. Sitting: Eldon, Eldon Jr., Robert Dean, Dale Eugene and Edna.

During the years at Creighton Brothers we had two daughters born - MaryEtta on December 7, 1944 and Ruby Arlene on January 7, 1946. Our third daughter was born after we moved to the Pringle Farm - LeAnna on August 18, 1948. The three girls were all born in Warsaw, Indiana, and the total cost for all three (delivery and pre-natal care) amounted to $150. How costs changed from when the doctor had his own hospital! Dale Eugene was born at the Elkhart Hospital May 9, 1952, and the pre-natal and hospital costs were over $200. Robert Dean was born June 5, 1953, at the new Goshen Hospital with the costs amounting to over $300. The next year Eldon Jr. was born May 19, 1954, also in the Goshen Hospital with pre-natal and hospital costs over $400.

When Eldon Jr. was two years old he was severely burned with hot popcorn grease. He still has scars on his chest. The corn popper was put on the burner and the heat turned on. My wife left the kitchen for a few minutes while Jr. was in the kitchen by himself. He reached up to get hold of the popper handle and pulled it down dumping the hot grease on his chest. He started to scream and screamed all the way to the Goshen Hospital where in minutes they had the pain under control. He had a few skin grafts on his chest. He had very little grease in his face.

Edna and the girls took care of the breeder hens that I had in my big laying house. Edna did this with few complaints while I was traveling all over the USA selling and installing new poultry equipment. The girls and boys all grew up during this period without a father at home most of the time.

The Hostetler family. Photo taken at a reunion August 1, 2004.

This is why I left my work when Edna became aware of a health problem. She did such an outstanding work taking care of the home while I was busy on the road, sometimes gone for two weeks. During her illness it was a time for reflection, and I became aware of what she must have done. I pray that she was rewarded for her dedication to the family. I ask God to bless her for being an understanding wife.

MaryEtta married Ray Yoder from Wooster, Ohio, and had two children, Edward Ray and Denise. Ruby Arlene married Marvin Wittmer and also had two children, Kelvin and Corina. LeAnna married Lamar Hochstetler and had two boys, Zebulon and Adam. Dale married Pamela Lambright and had two boys, Joshua and Andrew. Robert married Angelika Jende from Germany and had two boys, Lukas and Philip. Eldon Jr. married Pauline Wennerstrom, and they have no children.

I want to give a BIG THANK YOU to Norman Kauffmann who was in charge of the Shipshewana Project. He was faced with a big project that was going to cost millions of dollars, but with few dollars to work with. He first contacted a State agency that gave grants to certain groups like those that wanted to build bike paths. He checked to see if some of these funds were available for a car museum if the operations were under a 501(c)3.

They assured him money could be available for that type of a request. Shipshewana forwarded the necessary documents asking for $3,500,000 to get the project started, and were assured the request was not out of line. When all the promises were over, in the end the State presented a grant of $500,000. They tried another year and ended up with $2,000,000 in grants from the State. Four years of time was used just to get the amount needed for the outside shell of the building. Norman wanted to be in charge of the inside completion. By this time he had used most of his patience just to get the money for the outside shell.

When we were ready to start ground preparation, we were told someone had reported the project to the Detroit Army Corps of Engineers to investigate if there was any wet lands. They sent a person to meet with us at the location. When he drove up, the first words out of his mouth were, "I don't care who you are, Wal-Mart or any other big firm, if I find any wetlands here you can't build at this location." This was early in the morning and I have to give him credit that he was equipped to check all of our already checked points on wet land size and depth. As time went on he started to back down when we gave him no reason to get mad. The State had already checked the total area and knew the depth of wet lands at each flag. He finally agreed that we had done a good and complete check at every flag location.

By mid-afternoon he put his equipment back in the truck and said what the State had done was correct and if we removed muck at several locations and filled in with good ground and packed it, that it would qualify to build upon. We knew we were close at a few spots, but by us not saying anything he was ready to give us the "go ahead".

Norman asked me if I would consider using my endowment money to level the 18 acres. We hired McKibben Brothers, Inc. to remove the wet land soil area and use the high grounds to fill in the low area. After all grounds were leveled, drainage work had to be completed.

The underground heating system required digging all of the front and back of the parking areas and placing underground pipes. The trench was 6' wide and about that deep. There were three lines out beside each other and three lines returning back to a header pipe going along the east side, turning and going along the south side, then turning again along the west side. There were six trenches in front and eight trenches in the back parking lot.

When the State granted their $2,000,000 for putting up the outside shell, John Thomson of LaPorte, Indiana, was to oversee that part of the project. He got into health problems and was not able to complete the project. Bob White was hired by Maust Architect in Goshen, Indiana, to complete the total project according to their prints.

During this period that we were waiting for the town of Shipshewana to get a museum built, we attended many car shows. We took our 1942 Hudson Woodie to the Gilmore Car Show at Hickory Corners, Michigan. We won first in the class and the People's Choice awards.

Michael Spezia, Executive Director, asked us if we would consider loaning them some of our restored Hudsons. I told him I would if he would keep them in a controlled temperature room. He assured me he could do this. They came and looked at all of my collection and selected twenty-two of my cars and started to move them into a room by themselves. When I walked into the room, I couldn't believe these were my cars - they were so much better looking than when they were in my chicken house!

Because many persons came to Gilmore to select cars for their invited car shows, they could see our Hudsons and would ask how to get in touch with us to get us to bring one or two of our best Hudsons to their shows. Usually it was the special Cord or Packard cars that won "People's Choice" or "Best of Show" awards at these invited shows. Then the totally restored Hudsons started to win "Best of Show" and "People's Choice" awards. The Hudson Motor Car Company had 170 color combinations available if the customer was interested in a color combination no one else had and would pay the extra cost involved. Because of the recognition at shows, Hudson cars sky-rocketed in demand and prices increased the last couple of years.

Some models, restored to #1 condition, are selling for over $200,000. Some of the first cars we purchased for $7,500 are now selling for $75,000. We became very good friends of Michael and Ann Spezia so it wasn't easy to take those twenty-two Hudsons away from Gilmore after the museum in Shipshewana was ready.

Summary of Museum Milestones

July 16, 1992	Bought 8 acres on State Road 5 in Shipshewana at auction.
July 16, 1997	Bought 10 acres on State Road 5 in Shipshewana at auction.
December 1997	Contacted Norman Kauffmann about the Town of Shipshewana putting up a building for our Hudsons if we would donate them the land for a museum.
August 14, 2002	Governor Frank O'Bannon in Shipshewana to award $500,000 grant money from the federally funded transportation enhancements grants.
May 21, 2003	Purchased 5.67 acres just north of the 18 acres, behind Motel 8.
November 1, 2004 to March 17, 2006	McKibben Brothers, Inc. mowed, removed trees, leveled land.
February 25, 2005	Donated 18 acres to Town of Shipshewana.
August 25, 2005	Ground breaking ceremony.
Summer 2006	Started construction on building.
July 27, 2007	Hudson-Essex-Terraplane Club private tour of the museum.
September 4, 2007	Museum opened to the public.
October 5, 2007	Grand Opening of all buildings: Motel and Indoor Water Park; Town Center - Visitors' Center; Hudson Museum; and Expo. Center.

Ground breaking ceremony held August 25, 2005. Left to right: Kevin Carlson, Dean Morgan, Eldon and Esta Hostetler, and Roger Yoder, Shipshewana Town Council President.

The front view of the Shipshewana Town Center housing the Hostetler Hudson Auto Museum as it appeared at the grand opening in October 2007.

When I started putting my life's story on tape (as I remembered), it wasn't long until I found I always missed many things that happened and wasn't getting it recorded in the time sequence. This made a problem to relocate and insert events. So I started to write everything out on paper. Julie Wolfe in Shipshewana, Indiana, helped correct my spelling and language usage. I have to give her much credit for making my story readable.

Ginger Bush took my writings and typed them out on her computer, retyping many things because of all the changes I made at times after checking back and finding the correct time something happened. Ginger retyped and always did it with no complaints. I would make additions where needed and removed some. Her pleasant way of answering the phone has been a great help in our Ziggity office. May God bless her in the years ahead.

John Frederich at Creighton Brothers was a person that also became a great help and friend after I got into making automatic feeders and waterers. Creightons were always ready to test new products and give good advice if it needed further improvements. John was someone from whom I could always get good sound advice. I was very fortunate to have had him for my boss at Creighton Brothers the first several years of my life away from home. He was a person that had a talent to get along with everyone.

Howard Brembeck was a major stock owner of Chore-Time Equipment, Milford, Indiana. I became acquainted with Howard through John Holton, president of Anderson Box Company. Howard was sales manager for the hog feeders of Star Tank and Boat Co., Goshen, Indiana. Chore-Time Equipment was moved from Alliance, Ohio, to Milford, Indiana, because of Howard's work with Star Tank and Boat Co. Howard had a very good sales background along with a lot of common sense. He was able to get persons to make the best product possible made at a reasonable cost.

Forrest Ramser was one of the Chore-Time owners and Howard's partner. I worked mostly with him the first year getting production started. He was an energetic young person that kept things moving along. He was good at keeping employees happy with their work.

The twenty years I spent at Chore-Time Equipment was a great learning experience in introducing new products. I found a formula that worked. It was one that I needed to keep in mind when I showed something new the first time. When most poultrymen see the totally new products, their first reaction can be in three categories. Twenty-five percent will look at the product and say, "Whoever made this doesn't know anything about poultry equipment requirements." The next twenty-five percent will look at the same equipment and say, "This is a totally new approach, I think I might try." These are the only ones you can count on to try the product, so be prepared for them to try it for a trial sale. The other fifty percent are "from Missouri (*the show-me state*)", they will be convinced ten years later.

Chore-Time Equipment gave me almost complete freedom to introduce new concepts in equipment design. I drove the design engineers "up the wall" with my way of working. I would make the part without any prints and test it in the field for several months. Then I would bring it back in and set it on the drafting person's bench, asking him to make a set of prints for it. If you think this doesn't get under the design engineer's skin, just try it sometime! Howard Brembeck told every design engineer that I had complete freedom to do whatever I thought the industry needed. This made my job a fun one to work in. So all my life I didn't do much drafting on a table because I never had any teaching in it. I had a photographic mind so I knew what it would look like before I made it.

When I started Ziggity Systems, Inc. I found myself in need of having to get things on prints with dimensions and tolerances. Most all parts were plastic and required close tolerances. So I sat at one of these drafting tables and learned how to do this. Some of my early prints I would miss some of the really important dimensions. However, all of the early prints for single cavity molds for testing I did with the help of Dick Bender who made the molds. After the testing was done on the closed watering system, many drawings were needed to get multiple cavity molds made at Bender Mold in Mishawaka, Indiana. We had someone from Jayco help get prints made to get into production on our closed watering system.

When my son Dale was done with his military service, he agreed to help with production management. He proved to be good in production work. He sometimes got discouraged when production couldn't keep up with demands. The Poultry Industry has a habit of fluctuating during several years, so it was hard to know how much inventory to have at all times. He did very good at most times in keeping production up to demand.

It has been a great experience to introduce a patented closed hanging watering system to the contract broiler producers that has proven to be a big help in disease control in growing broilers. The last number of years made it possible to be able to purchase and restore Hudson cars that became quite valuable, which was a side benefit. Howard Brembeck always said, "If you make a good product and provide services, the rewards come automatically." I feel that God has rewarded me beyond words.

I have been blessed with the Indiana State Poultry Association Golden Egg Award for my contribution to the Poultry Industry. Also the D.C. "Doc" Daugherty Memorial Award for outstanding service and promotion of the National Hudson - Essex - Terraplane Club. A big award was given by Indiana Governor Mitchell E. Daniels, Jr. called the Sagamore of the Wabash Award, the State's highest civilian award, at the opening ceremony of

The Golden Egg Award

the Shipshewana Town Center covering the Visitors Bureau, Expo Center and Hudson Auto Museum.

During the years spent at Ziggity Systems, Inc., we had a great sales team that did an excellent job promoting our product. The personnel in the different areas in the office were equally great to work with. May God continue to give them good health to continue in their work. We lost Andrew Miller due to health problems. He was also a good person on our team for many years.

D.C. "Doc" Daugherty Memorial Award presented to us for outstanding service and promotion of the National Hudson - Essex - Terraplane Club.

— 138 —

Sagamore of the Wabash Award from Indiana Governor Mitchell E. Daniels, Jr. It was presented to me during the Grand Opening Ceremony of the Hudson Museum.

At 85 years of age, I can't expect too many more years to be here. When I think back to the training my father and mother gave me as the oldest child in the family - the oldest one was usually given early responsibilities looking after and doing adult things with the younger ones - I see it gave me good training for future years.

"Thanks for everything!"

May God bless all of you that read my life and thoughts.

— Eldon "Hot Ziggity" Hostetler

Hostetler's Hudson Auto Museum

Hostetler's Hudson Auto Museum is housed in the Shipshewana Town Center on State Road 5 on the south side of Shipshewana, Indiana. The address is 760 S. VanBuren Street, Shipshewana, Indiana 46565. The museum is open from 9 am to 5 pm daily all year long.

This collection of cars and trucks is the largest collection of Hudson, Essex, Terraplane, and Railton vehicles anywhere. For more information on the collection and the museum, go to *www.hostetlershudsons.com* or call 260-768-3021.

Car Photo Credits:
Car photos on pages 141-154, and 156-189 by Roy D. Query.
Car photo on page 155 by Melody DuVal.

Eldon and Esta Hostetler in one of their beloved Hudsons.

Photo by: Ken Dallison

Hudson Appendix

A model of the Hudson, "Doc" used in the popular movie "Cars" graced the foyer at the Shipshewana Town Center at the entrance to the Hostetler Hudson Car Museum during the time it was on loan.

1909 Hudson Model: 20

Engine:.................Atlas and later a Buda
Engine Size:............... 3¾" x   for 198 cid
Horsepower:... 20
Weight:..................................... 1,800 lbs
Wheelbase:.....................................100"
Cost:..$900

Production: 1,100 cars were shipped to dealers between July and December 1909.

Features: The company touted their first car as: "Strong - Speedy - Roomy - Stylish." It offered a 20 horsepower four-cylinder engine, a sliding-gear transmission and a leather-faced cone clutch.

History: Roy D. Chapin and Howard E. Detroit, formally associated with Chalmers-Detroit and Oldsmobile persuaded Joseph L. Hudson, founder of Hudson Department Stores, to invest $90,000 in the Hudson. They purchased the factory of the Aero Car Co. and the Seldon patent license of the Northern in January 1909. The first Hudson left the factory July 8, 1909, and by the following July 4,000 of these cars had been sold.

Context: The popularity of automobiling led to the development of special clothes for the sport and the ruddy-faced outdoor girl replaced the soft, pale Gibson fashions.

(Although built in 1909, this model is considered a 1910.)

On Oct. 20, 1990, Esta and I went to Sam Vaughan's car auction in Uncertain, Texas. He had been killed in a plane crash and all of his car collection had to be sold due to them all being mortgaged to a bank. He had 151 cars, trucks, and motorcycles. The only Hudson listed was this 1909 restored Hudson Roadster. Mr. Vaughan had purchased the Roadster from the Palace Museum located in Las Vegas, Nevada. The museum had purchased the 1909 Hudson at the Harrah's car auction. The Palace Museum restored it and displayed it several years before selling it to Sam Vaughan in 1988. We had to wait until the second day of the three day sale for it to come up for sale. I was able to purchase it for the money I had in mind. This added a very important car to my collection.

1911 Hudson Model: "33" Speedster

Engine:	Four-cylinder Continental*
Engine Size:	4" x 4½" for 226 cid
Horsepower:	33
Weight:	est. 1,800 lbs
Wheelbase:	114"
Cost:	N/A

Production: 1

Features: Custom built body, clutch faced with cork and enclosed in an oil bath.

History: When the Hudson Motor Car Company opened its first sales agency in Puerto Rico, this Speedster built on a race-car chassis, was used to promote Hudson sales there. The car was driven for several days at 60 mph to promote its reliability. It was subsequently parked, allowed to deteriorate, and then finally returned to the United States. It was restored to its present condition and acquired by Eldon Hostetler in 1991.

Context: Ray Harroun won the first Indianapolis 500 at a speed of 74.59 mph in the famed Marmon "Wasp" that was equipped with the first rear view mirror. Charles Kettering perfected the electric starter for the automobile which was introduced in the 1912 Cadillac.

* Continental Motors Corp. built a factory in Detroit in 1911 and became the exclusive engine supplier for Hudson.

I was at the Hershey, Pennsylvania Fall Antique Car Meet in 1987 when this Hudson Speedster was on display by Ken Shields Body Works located in St. Thomas, Pennsylvania. He had just completed a total restoration on the car for Dr. Warren D. Kistler located in Chambersburg, Pennsylvania. Dr. Kistler was on vacation in Puerto Rico when he met Efrain Latoni on the golf course. Mr. Latoni had three antique cars for sale: the 1911 Hudson Speedster, an early Pierce Arrow, and an early V12 Lincoln. Dr. Kistler purchased all three and had them returned to the states to be restored. I left word with Ken Shields that if the car ever came up for sale to call me. Several years later the doctor's wife filed for divorce, so Ken called me and I was able to purchase the Speedster on April 19, 1991.

1911 Hudson Model: Cabriolet Runabout

Engine:	L-head, four-cylinder
Engine Size:	4" x 4½"
Horsepower:	33
Weight:	N/A
Wheelbase:	N/A
Cost:	Under $2,000

Production: A gain of 42.4% over 1910 with an output of 6,486 for all models that year.

Features: The enclosed three-speed transmission was in a case which looped around the flywheel in a yoke manner. This was bolted to the engine to form what was termed "Virtually a unit power plant."

History: A custom body was made by Rawlinson in 1911 in London, England. The car was sold and driven in England until 1954. It was sold in the United States by Vintage Autos to Mr. Dan J. Bihler of Moundsville, West Virginia. Its current restoration was done by Milford Barker, of Havana, Florida. The car was later sold to Wayne Hadden of Cairo, Georgia. In 2004 the car was purchased in its restored condition and added to the Hostetler Collection. This is a most unusual car for 1911. The custom builder added a starter, coil distributors to the motor, and a twelve-volt electrical system.

Context: Air conditioning is invented. A new macadam track at the Indianapolis Speedway is inaugurated with a five-hundred-mile race, the first Indianapolis 500.

In 1911 Hudson shipped a chassis to London, England, to the Rawlinson Body Works at Grosvenor Square. The custom body builder added a 12 volt system with starter and generator. The car was sold and driven in England until 1954. Vintage Auto, located in London, sold it to Dan J. Bihler of Moundsville, West Virginia, who owned it until 1980 when he sold it to Milford Barker of Havana, Florida. He toured with it for several years and then sold it to Wayne Hadden of Cairo, Georgia from whom we purchased the car on October 6, 2004. It is an unusual car equipped with starter and electric lights.

1913 Hudson Model: Touring Car

```
Engine:...............................Four-cylinder
Engine Size:.......3¾" x 4½" for 198.8 cid
Horsepower:....................................20-25
Weight:..................................... 2,757 lbs
Wheelbase:...................................... 115"
Cost:..............................................$1,600
```

Production: N/A

Features: The Hudson four-cylinder engine was of the French Renault design. All the valves were on the right-hand side. Bore and stroke 3¾" x 4½", the displacement was 198.8 cubic inches and horsepower output was 20-25. The crankshaft was supported on two main bearings. The crankcase had integral walls which divided it into four compartments, one below each cylinder. The lubrication was by pump, of forced circulation splash system.

History: This was the first Hudson model to have an electric starter for the motor. It starts on twenty-four volts and changes to six volts after it's running. This car has an overdrive installed, thus is geared to run in traffic. The overdrive was made in El Cajon, California. It has done several tours: 1968 - New York, New York, to San Francisco, California; 1976 - Seattle, Washington to Philadelphia, Pennsylvania; and 1985 - Portland, Maine to Portland, Oregon. Stickers are on the windshield verifying these completed tours throughout the USA.

Context: The seventeenth amendment provides for the direct election of US senators.

This car was sold at a government auction in Salt Lake City, Utah. Merrill Maxfield owned a fleet of semi trucks and got into tax problems with no payment on road taxes. The government sold his collection of antique cars for tax collection. I bought two cars from his collection. He also had many Hudson parts that were sold. This Hudson Touring car was equipped with a Kettering self-starting system, one that shifted from six volts to twenty-four volts to start, then back to six volts after running and becoming a generator. Only Cadillac and Hudson used this in 1913. Merrill Maxfield took part in many tours across the USA with this car.

1915 Hudson Model: Six-40

This car was purchased November 14, 2005 from Alex McCommas, of Tyler, Texas. He toured with the car in Texas and had restored the car to make that possible. I haven't been able to contact him to get more background on the car.

Engine:...................	Six-cylinder Hudson
Engine Size:..........	3½" x 5" for 288.5 cid
Horsepower:...	40
Weight:.....................................	2,977 lbs
Wheelbase:.......................................	123"
Cost:...	$1,750

Production: N/A

Features: Appearance changes included enclosed hinges on all models and a reshaped radiator with smooth curves.

History: Hudson was strictly a manufacturer of six-cylinder automobiles in 1914 and while the new Six-40 Series was larger than the four-cylinder models they replaced, their prices were reduced. The new engine's dimensions of 3½" bore and 5" stroke pointed toward future American practice and offered both better fuel economy and more power than the old four-cylinder. The president of Hudson was Roy D. Chapin.

Context: The Ford Motor Company announced an eight-hour working day, paid at a minimum of $5 per day. The first World War began when Austro-Hungary mobilized against Serbia after Archduke Franz Ferdinand was assassinated in Sarajevo. The USA and Panama signed the Panama Canal Treaty.

1916 Hudson Model: Limousine Four-Door

```
Engine:................................ Six-cylinder
Engine Size:..........3½" x 5" for 288.6 cid
Horsepower:......................................N/A
Weight:..................................... 3,535 lbs
Wheelbase:.....................................123"
Cost:............................................$2,450
```

Production: An increase of 100.2% over 1915 producing 25,772 for all models. The increase was due to the Super Six series.

Features: The carburetor air could now be adjusted by a control on the instrument board. The gasoline tank capacity was increased to 14 gallons. For easier lubrication the clutch grease cup was projected through the floor.

History: Hudson adopted a new policy that rejected annual models and was committed to a formula of on-going series with minimal changes made at discretionary intervals. This is a very unusual and rare car to have in a collection. For many years it was owned by Bobby Barlow. Jimmy Alsbrook of Florence, South Carolina, purchased it from the Barlow estate. Robert Kavanah of Montreal, Quebec, Canada, later bought it. He brought it to Hershey, Pennsylvania, where it was purchased in October of 2006 for the Hostetler Collection.

Context: Domestic commerce generates $45 billion and exports top $8 billion. The self-service concept in retailing is invented by the Piggly Wiggly chain of grocery stores. Boeing Aircraft Company designs and produces its first model, the biplane.

We saw this car in a car sales lot in Hershey, Pennsylvania in October of 2006. It had been brought from Montreal, Canada, by Robert Kavanah who had purchased the Hudson from Jimmy Alsbrook of Florence, South Carolina. Mr. Alsbrook had purchased the car earlier from Bobby Barlow, also from Florence, South Carolina. This is a very rare car. I saw one of these fully restored in a small town museum near Melbourne, Australia in 1994.

1917 Hudson Model: Shaw Special Race Car

In 1917 Hudson made ten race engines with a patented balanced crankshaft. They had drilled the crankshaft also for forced lubrication and had special connecting rods, special cams and timing gears. In 1918 Horace Shaw of Rochester, New York, and individual car builder and driver, acquired one of these engines and proceeded to build a Hudson race car. This car was driven on race tracks in the eastern parts of the USA. It was found stored in a shed in northeastern New York State and was purchased by Tom Rowe of Rock Island, Illinois. Al Prueitt and Sons did the restoration project. It has been certified by several auto organizations: the AACA issued No. 72, the crankcase is marked No. 1, the AAA No. 123. The chassis is special. The engine is a six cylinder 292 overhead intake, two updraft carburetors and has a 96" wheelbase.

Engine:	Six-cylinder Continental
Engine Size:	292 cid
	with two updraft carburetors
Horsepower:	N/A
Weight:	N/A
Wheelbase:	96"
Cost:	N/A

Production: Hudson built ten race engines.

Features: Two updraft carburetors and chrome alloy engine block.

History: Hudson built ten race engines in 1917. Horace Shaw of Rochester, New York, acquired one of these engines and built this car on a Duesenberg chassis. Reportedly, the Shaw Special raced mostly in the eastern United States. Ralph Mulford won at Omaha in 1917 with the same Super-Six Hudson engine and possibly a similar appearing car. This car has been certified for authenticity by the Antique Automobile Club of America (AACA).

Context: There were almost five million motor vehicles in this country accounting for 88% of all vehicles in the world in 1917. Two million vehicles were built here that year and the average price was $720. Woodrow Wilson's famous phrase: "The world must be made safe for democracy," was coined in his declaration of war against Germany.

1921 Hudson Model: Opera Coupe

A doctor in Evansville, Indiana, had purchased this car new. It has an all aluminum body. We think it is one of the first years Biddle and Smart made bodies for Hudson; they made only all aluminum bodied cars at first for Hudson. We purchased this car from Marion Whitsett north of Sellersburg, Indiana. He had the car many years before restoring it. We purchased it July 16, 1988. This car is somewhat special due to exposed wood around the front and the windows. The car has a special heater setup located in the floor of the car.

Engine:................................	Six-cylinder
Engine Size:..........	3½" x 5" at 288.6 cid
Horsepower:...	70
Weight:.....................................	3,620 lbs
Wheelbase:.....................	125½" to 126"
Cost:...	$2,275

Production: Limited.

Features: Heavier fenders. A ball control replaced the H-slot plate at the bottom of the shift level which made gear shifting easier. The accelerator pedal was moved to the right of the brake pedal.

History: This car was purchased new by a doctor in Evansville, Indiana. It had a custom aluminum body. The builder of this body is unknown. The car was purchased for the Hostetler collection in 1988 from Mr. Whitsett who had restored it in 1985.

Context: The first electronically-transmitted photograph is sent by Western Union. The idea for a facsimile transmission was first proposed by Scottish clock maker Alexander Bain in 1843. Writing under the pen name of Agatha Christie, Mary Clarissa Miller launches an enormously successful career as a mystery writer. In the annals of fashion, Chanel No. 5 makes a splash, becoming the world's best-selling perfume.

1922 Hudson Model: Essex

Engine:......................F-head, Inline Four	
Engine Size:...........3-3/8" x 5 for 180 cid	
Horsepower:.....................................18.2	
Weight:.................................... 2,600 lbs	
Wheelbase:..................................108½"	
Cost:..$1,045	

I had a picture of this car for many years, mounted on wood, hanging in my collection room. The picture had a lady standing beside the car which had a California license plate number. The car was listed for sale at the Auburn Auction and was scheduled to sell the day after I saw it. I purchased a bidder's tag and went back the next day to see what it might cost to own it. The Essex had been owned by Ralph Levin. The car was tour driven in California for many years before being sold at the Auburn Auction.

Production: N/A

Features: Essex, like Hudson, offered two versions of the 1922 models with the first type phasing in the new drum shaped fuel tank. A new wider body was adopted for the touring car with wider doors and front hinges.

History: Hudson and Essex were merged into a single company in 1922 and shares in the new company were listed on the New York Stock Exchange. The Essex line for 1922 was best remembered for its new coach model which proved to be a key catalyst speeding up the demise of the open cars as the predominate body style among American automobiles. Alfred P. Sloan later wrote that the introduction of the Essex coach was "an event which was to profoundly influence the fortunes of Pontiac, Chevrolet and the Model T." Although its styling was less than sensational, the low price of the coach model assured its success.

Context: The Lincoln Memorial was dedicated in Washington D.C. The President was Warren G. Harding. Mussolini marched on Rome and formed a Fascist Government.

1925 Hudson Model: Essex Roadster Convertible

```
Engine:................................ Six-cylinder
Engine Size:...................................... N/A
Horsepower:..................................... N/A
Weight:............................................. N/A
Wheelbase:....................................... N/A
Cost:................................................. N/A
```

Production: No Roadsters were produced during this year. In all, only five factory models of the Super-Six series were produced. The Hudson Motor Car Company did move into the No. 3 spot in the industry though.

Features: This Roadster has a custom body built by Johnson & Smith, of New Zealand. It was also called the "2 Seater," and has a "dickey" seat, meaning that it can carry three people. It has small lamps on the front fenders, and a plated radiator shell. This car is also a right-hand drive.

History: In the 1960s an American bought the car in New Zealand to take part in a Classic Road Rally being held in New Zealand. It was brought back to the States and later purchased in 1999 for the Hostetler collection. At purchase time it had only 26,047 miles on it. This rare Essex is the only one known to exist.

Context: The Roaring '20s are in full swing as a new dance music is beginning to emerge as a form distinct from jazz. Baseball player Lou Gehrig joins the New York Yankees.

Hudson Motor Company sold chassis to custom body builders in many parts of the world. This Essex Sports Roadster had a body made for it by Johnson and Smith located at Christchurch, New Zealand. This rare Essex is the only one that exists. In 1960 someone took a left-hand drive Ford from California to New Zealand to take part in a country tour. When he arrived he found the tour rules required him to have a right-hand drive car to be able to enter the Classic Road Rally. The American traded his Ford with a local museum for this 1925 Essex and then participated in the Road Rally. When the Rally was completed he liked driving the car so much he paid to have it brought back to California. It was driven in tours and shown at car shows. It ended up in several states before we saw a sale bill listing it near Denver, Colorado. I purchased it over the phone during sale day, September 18, 1999, from Ferrell Auction Company of Loveland, Colorado. The Essex had only 26,047 original miles on it.

1927 Hudson Model: Fire Engine

Engine:	F-head, six-cylinder
Engine Size:	3½" x 5" at 288.6 cid
Horsepower:	29.4
Weight:	N/A
Wheelbase:	127-7/8"
Cost:	N/A

Production: Only a Hudson limousine chassis was used. The rest was custom made.

Features: A 500 gallon per minute Northern Pump was installed. It carries a priming tank of water. The connections are large so the suction hose can hook up to the hydrants or take water from any lake or tank, etc.

History: In Alden, Minnesota, in 1927, due to the fact that firefighters did not have a pumper, they were unable to rescue a woman and a child from a very bad fire. A local Hudson dealer provided a new, long wheelbase Hudson complete. The dealer's body shop and the local volunteer firefighters built the "Flintstone" in Alden. It was in daily use from 1927 through 1958. It was in good condition when it was retired, but deteriorated from exposure through the years. Restoration by Bruce Mori-Kubo was done in 1980. The fire engine was purchased in restored condition in 2002 for the Hostetler collection.

Context: TV is demonstrated for the first time, but full-scale development is delayed nearly two decades. Babe Ruth sets a new record, hitting sixty home runs in a season, a record that was to stand for thirty years.

Hudson Motor Company never made a fire truck. This fire truck was made by a welding shop in Alden, Minnesota, in 1927. They purchased a Hudson long wheelbase car and removed the body and proceeded to build a fire truck. Why a Hudson car? The Hudson overhead intake motor with large radiator was powerful enough and kept cool sitting stationary to power a water pump that pumped 500 gallons per minute when set in second gear and forty miles per hour on the speedometer. This fire truck was used until 1958 when it was retired. It sat for many years until 1980 when Bruce Mar-Kubo, a Hudson Club member, found it for sale. He restored it to its present condition. In September of 2002, his wife sold it to us following Bruce's death.

1928 Hudson Model: Victoria Coach

Engine:................................. Six-cylinder
Engine Size:........... 3½" x 5" at 288.6 cid
Horsepower:..................................... 29.4
Weight:...................................... 3,710 lbs
Wheelbase:................................... 127½"
Cost:... $1,650

Production: N/A

Features: This car was Murphy designed and Biddle & Smart built the body. All Hudson models now came with the new Triplex "shatterproof" windshield glass. Lacquer paints which matched the upper body colors replaced the black paint used on fenders and chassis sheet metal used on all Hudsons. This car has two side mounts and Landau arms.

History: Records show there is only one other Victoria car left. It has wood wheels and no Landau arms. In 1966 this unrestored car was purchased along with a large collection of extra parts for this car.

Context: At age 26, Margaret Mead, one of the best-known writers in anthropology, publishes *Coming of Age in Samoa*. At the end of 44 years of work, the Oxford English Dictionary appears. Republican Herbert Hoover, Secretary of Commerce, is elected 31st President of the United States. In the midst of Prohibition, physicians write prescriptions for whisky as a therapeutic substance.

This is a show car designed by Murphy in California. It was made by Biddle & Smart of Massachusetts. This car was bought by John J. Struthers of Highland Park, Illinois, in an estate sale in Upper Michigan. He was going to restore it, but never got started on it. He decided to sell the car, along with all the extra parts he had collected for the restoration. I heard about the car and decided to buy it and all the parts in December of 1996. We didn't get started restoring it until later. This car is admired by most women.

1928 Hudson Model: Sedan Convertible

Engine:...............................	Six-cylinder
Engine Size:...........	3½" x 5" at 288.6 cid
Horsepower:.......................................	N/A
Weight:.....................................	3,645 lbs
Wheelbase:..............................	127-3/8"
Cost:...	$5,000

Production: 4

Features: The Hudson Motor Car Company had the Walter M. Murphy Company build four cars for the Hudson executives. The bodies were totally aluminum with retractable tops.

History: The executives drove these cars for several years before selling them as used cars to customers. Two of the four cars are in the Hostetler Collection. The Hudson Motor Company began to attach the year to its cars such as "1928 models."

Context: Josef Stalin implements the first Five-Year Plan and begins to collectivize agriculture in the USSR. The second Winter Olympics in St. Moritz, Switzerland, held at a ski resort, were marred by bad weather. The culprit was the foehn, a strong wind that carried with it warm air, causing temperatures to soar above 75° F (24° C) some afternoons. Many events were rescheduled, and the 10,000-meter speed skating event was cancelled. Some books list American Irving Jaffee, who held the lead after the first run, as the winner. Also, German athletes returned. They'd been banned from Olympic competition following World War I.

Walter Murphy was a Hudson car distributor in California. He was also a designer and custom car builder. In 1928 Hudson sent several chassis to him, asking him to make convertible four-door sedan bodies for them. I have two of them in this collection. They aren't quite the same in two areas: the hood and the running boards. Both cars are all aluminum with cloth tops that are retractable. Both cars had the same dash design. This car was in Harrah's Collection from 1966 to 1985 when it was sold to the Rupert Beer Company. It ended up with Mark Smith, an antique car dealer in Skippack, Pennsylvania. I purchased it from him in the fall of 1998. The two Murphy cars are unusual.

1928 Hudson Model: Essex Coach

```
Engine:................................ Six-cylinder
Engine Size:. 2-11/16" x 4¼" at 144.7 cid
Horsepower:................17.3 at 4,000 rpm
Weight:......................................2,560 lbs
Wheelbase:....................................110½"
Cost:...............................................$735
```

Production: 229,887

Features: The beauty of the Essex Coach drew the attention of many women, but it was also roomy and comfortable for the entire family. Its seats were high-backed, form-fitting, and covered in fine quality materials. All its lines were very graceful. Among some of the other features which enticed the family were: the controls were very handy, the doors were weather stripped, and the floors were matted. Four-wheel brakes by Bendix became standard, and many optional colors were offered.

History: The 1928 Essex Coach was purchased at a farm sale near Kendallville, Indiana, in July of 2002. There isn't any information on who the original owner was when the Essex was new. Restoration took place from 2006 to 2007. It was done by the Appenzeller Brothers in Milford, Indiana. The Hudson Motor Car Company was number four in car production in 1928.

Context: In the midst of Prohibition, physicians write prescriptions for whiskey as a therapeutic substance.

This 1928 Essex Coach was purchased near Kendallville, Indiana, at a farm sale in July of 2002. We weren't able to find out who had purchased the Essex new. We started to have it restored by the Appenzeller Brothers in 2006 and it took until a year later to get this small car finished. Production numbers in Essex model cars were 229,887 units. Hudson Company was number four in car manufacturing numbers in 1928.

1928 Hudson Model: Four-Door Town Car

This is the only Town Car known to exist that had a Hudson chassis. This car body was designed and made by Walter M. Murphy Body Company of Pasadena, California. The car was made for Mrs. Fredrich William Schmacker, wife of the Patent King of Columbus, Ohio. Her brother worked in the office of Hudson Motor Car Company in Detroit, Michigan. She wanted the Town Car to be a Hudson. Her brother had the Hudson Company lengthen a chassis to fit the Town Car design. Mr. Schmacher did not want the Town Car to look like a Hudson, so Murphy made a new style hood ornament. The total cost of the Murphy custom made Hudson Town Car was $14,500 in 1928.

Engine:	Six-cylinder
Engine Size:	3½" x 5" at 288.6 cid
Horsepower:	N/A
Weight:	N/A
Wheelbase:	N/A
Cost:	$14,500

Production: 1

Features: It has a Super-Six chassis. The body was built by Walter M. Murphy Body Company of Pasadena, California. The instruction for building the body was that it not resemble a Hudson. It was very luxuriously finished and equipped.

History: The car was built for Mrs. Fredrich William Schmacher. She was the wife of the patent medicine king of Columbus, Ohio. The Hudson chassis was acquired through her brother who was an official at the Hudson Motor Car Company. This is a one-of-a-kind town car. During the period it was owned by Mrs. Schmacher, it was always driven by a chauffeur and never left outside.

Context: Walter E. Diemer, an accountant for the Fleer Chewing Gum Company, accidentally invented bubble gum while experimenting during his spare time with recipes for a chewing gum base. Gloria Swanson, the glamorous queen of silent movies, formed her own production company with backing from her lover, Joseph P. Kennedy, making *Sadie Thompson* and then the disastrous *Queen Kelly*.

1929 Hudson Model: Essex Speedabout, Boatail

Engine:................................. Six-cylinder
Engine Size:.. N/A
Horsepower:..............55 hp at 3,600 rpm
Weight...................................... 2,500 lbs
Wheelbase:.. N/A
Cost:...$695

Very few of these high priced Biddle and Smart, all aluminum custom body, Essex Boatail Speedabouts were ever sold. They were only made to order. We know of only one other one left and that one is in the Reno Museum. This car was owned by Maruice J. Curran III, of Chestnut Hill, Massachusetts. He placed the car in the Larry Anders Museum in Brookline, Massachusetts in 1972. It was light brown with darker fenders. They had a sale. It was sold to Dave Mange who owned it several years and placed it in the Owls Head Museum in Maine. It was later sold to MBNA Marketing Systems. They brought it to the Hershey Antique Car Meet to sell in 1996. Glen Weeks of Frankfurt, Illinois, purchased the car and restored it. In 1998 he brought the car to the Auburn Auction to sell with a reserve. It did not bring his price. I had told him the day before what my highest offer was, so after the sale he called me and said I should bring my trailer and I could have the car. So in September of 1998 we purchased it.

Production: 5

Features: The custom, all aluminum body was built by Biddle and Smart of Amesbury, Massachusetts. The boatail body had a rumble seat. Containing special gear ratios and an overdrive transmission, it could reach about 80 mph. All of the five cars made were used as show cars, and of the five produced we only know of one other one that has survived.

History: The sales of the Essex increased so that in 1929 the Hudson Motor Car Company was in third place in overall sales. The Hostetler collection purchased this car in 1998.

Context: In the fight for control of the bootleg liquor trade in Prohibition Chicago, seven gang members are killed in the St. Valentine's Day Massacre. Clarence Birdseye offers his quick-frozen foods to the public. Birdseye got the idea during fur-trapping expeditions to Labrador in 1912 and 1916, where he saw the natives use freezing to preserve foods.

1929 Hudson Model: R Coupe

This is one of the first cars we bought, in August of 1987. It had been purchased from the Olds Museum in Lansing, Michigan, by a mother for her son to make into a street rod. Instead the son joined the Army to save money to do it. However, he liked the service so much he then decided to make a career out of it. The parents then placed an ad to sell the car. We checked out the coupe and decided to buy it. In 1992 we took the car to Appenzeller Brothers for restoration.

Engine:	Six-cylinder
Engine Size:	3½" x 5" at 288.5 cid
Horsepower:	92 at 3,200 rpm
Weight:	3,610 lbs
Wheelbase:	122½"
Cost:	$1,195

Production: N/A

Features: In an era of custom bodied vehicles, this car was finished by Hudson.

History: The 1929 Models were introduced with 64 improvements including double-action shock absorbers, electric gauges, and improved four-wheel mechanical brakes. This color combination was typical of the Hudson built during this period. This car was added to the Hostetler collection in 1991, and restored by the Appenzeller Brothers in 1994.

Context: Herbert Hoover continued to speak optimistically about the economy, asserting that the "fundamental business of the country is on a sound and prosperous basis." But, in fact, the Great Depression of the 1930s had begun. National income statistics showed that 60% of US citizens had an annual income of less than $2,000, the estimated minimum to sustain a family with the bare necessities of life. We were singing "Singin' in the Rain."

1929 Hudson Model: R Convertible Coupe

Engine:	Six-cylinder
Engine Size:	3½" x 5" for 288.5 cid
Horsepower:	92 at 3,200 rpm
Weight:	3,580 lbs
Wheelbase:	122½"
Cost:	$1,450

We purchased this car at an auction conducted by the US Government due to taxes owed. Merrill Maxfield bought the Hudson Roadster in California and drove it across the steep mountains in the west. The restoration shop in California had changed the crankshaft dip system to a pressure system. When the car was driven over the mountains at a steep angle the oil pump failed to pick up oil. He burned out several rod bearings before he was aware of a problem. We purchased the Roadster in 1988. This is a Briggs bodied car with a converted oil crankshaft.

Production: N/A, very limited.

Features: This car was bodied by the Briggs Body Company.

History: The Hudson Motor Car Company offered a number of custom-bodied cars in 1929. This particular model was built by Briggs, a company that made bodies for several manufacturers, including the Ford Motor Car Company. This particular car was originally purchased at a public sale held by the US Government and was added to the Hostetler collection in 1988.

Context: On October 29, Black Tuesday, a record 16,410,030 shares were sold on Wall Street at any price, and by December 1, the New York Stock Exchange had dropped in value by $26 billion. Herbert Hoover had been inaugurated in March and his political slogan "A chicken in every pot and a car in every garage," continued to reverberate across the country, but hard times were here to stay. In New York City, women earned $33.50 for a 50-hour work week.

1929 Hudson Model: L Club Sedan

Pete Booz of California had this car from 1988 to 1993. We purchased it from him in 1993 and had the Appenzeller Brothers start to restore it in 1999. This car was the biggest car Hudson had for sale with a 129 inch wheelbase and weighing 4,140 pounds. This was a custom bodied car by Biddle and Smart made in Amesbury, Massachusetts. They made, and shipped by rail, 400 custom bodies a week during the 1920's to the Hudson Motor Car Company. This is a car that is recognized as a true classic car by both AACA and CCCA Clubs.

```
Engine:................................ Six-cylinder
Engine Size:..........3½" x 5" for 288.5 cid
Horsepower:..................92 at 3,200 rpm
Weight:.................................... 4,140 lbs
Wheelbase:.....................................139"
Cost:...........................................$1,850
```

Production: Limited production, approximately six survive.

Features: This is the longest and also the heaviest Hudson ever built. It offers four-wheel mechanical brakes and an electric lock anti-theft device.

History: The Model L epitomizes the Greater Hudson line introduced this year. The coach work is by Biddle & Smart, a well-known and well-respected coach builder in Amesburg, Massachusetts. They specialized in horse-drawn hearses and their heritage is evident in the tasteful finish of this automobile. The Model L is the only full-classic Hudson automobile recognized by the Classic Car Club of America.

Context: Herbert Hoover was inaugurated in March, interest rates rose to 15% in April, and the stock market reached a high of 381.17 in September, but crashed on October 29, sending this country into the Great Depression. The flapper fad faded with the onset of economic hard times.

1929 Hudson Model: Essex Dover U.S. Mail Truck

Engine:	Six-cylinder
Engine Size:	3½" x 5" for 288.6 cid
Horsepower:	92 hp at 3,200 rpm
Weight:	2,910 lbs
Wheelbase:	N/A
Cost:	$895

Production: 500

Features: This car shows the adaptation of Essex fenders, running board and headlamps. It has a radiator which is distinctively Dover with horizontal rather than vertical shutters. The payload capacity has a 3/4 ton maximum, which includes the driver. The body is steel-sheathed with wood fillers.

History: The United States Postal Service bought these to transport and deliver mail. Being so durable, the USPS used some Dovers well into the 1950s. The Dover vehicles were pulled from the market in 1930 or 1931. Only a few have survived. This car was found in 1970 and restored. It was loaned to the Auburn Museum for a period of time. In 1993 it was purchased for the Hostetler collection.

Context: On Wall Street, the stock market crashes on October 29, and $30 billion disappears, ushering in the Great Depression. Penicillin, discovered by Alexander Fleming, is first used to fight infection, a landmark in the history of medicine.

In 1929 the US Postal Department purchased 500 Dover Mail Trucks from the Hudson Motor Car Company. All commercial trucks made by Hudson during 1929 and 1930 were called Dover. Nobody has been able to tell me why this was started and then quickly stopped. Harrah's found this truck in the state of Wyoming in a field. They bought the truck, completed a total replacement of the wood body and had it on display until the auction. George Crocker purchased it at Harrah's sale. He kept it for several years and then brought it to the Kruse Auction to sell, but didn't bring his reserve. Auburn Museum made a deal with him to have it on display at the Natmus Museum for a small benefit to Mr. Crocker. The museum manager left after a few years and a new one was hired. The new manager was not going to pay anything to anyone to have a car placed at the museum. So George Crocker advertised the mail truck in Old Cars Weekly. I saw the ad and decided to go look at the vehicle. I first told Mr. Crocker I was going to do this and did not want him to sell before he heard back from me. The museum was not going to let me in when they heard why I was there. They called Mr. Crocker and tried to buy the truck before they let me in to see it. He told them he had promised me first chance so they then let me in. After seeing the mail truck I was sure I wanted to buy it.

1929 Hudson Model: Dual Cowl, Four-Door, Sport Phaeton

Engine:...................	F-head, Six-cylinder
Engine Size:..........	3½" x 5" for 288.5 cid
Horsepower:..............	92 hp at 3,200 rpm
Weight:....................................	2,940 lbs
Wheelbase:.......................................	139"
Cost:..........................	$1,300 cut to $965

Production: 17

Features: The five-passenger Phaeton was on the Hudson Great Eight Model T chassis. The body was built by Biddle & Smart of Massachusetts.

History: This car is one of the seven left today in the world out of only seventeen ever produced.

Context: Penicillin, discovered by Alexander Fleming, is first used to fight infection, a landmark in the history of medicine. In literature, William Faulkner publishes *The Sound and the Fury*, and Ernest Hemingway pens *A Farewell to Arms*. The Museum of Modern Art opens with an exhibition of paintings by Van Gogh and impressionists such as Cezanne.

We purchased the 1929 Dual Cowl Hudson from Jack Miller at the end of October 1992. The Dual Cowl Hudson was owned by a company near Ypsilanti, Michigan. Two brothers owned this company and legal problems developed between them so Jack was given custody of the car until differences settled. He told me on one of my visits that the car would be for sale when the money ran out. A year and a half later I received a phone call asking if I was still interested in the Dual Cowl. This is a rare model, so I said I was. He told me the price and we ended up purchasing it. We kept it several years before having it restored. I was not sure what color to make it, but after I found the orange/yellow Hudson ad, I knew what color it should be. This car is on the same chassis as the Club Sedan Model by Biddle & Smart. Not many of these models were made in the first place.

1930 Hudson Model: T Coupe with Rumble Seat

Engine:................L-head, Eight-cylinder
Engine Size:......... 2¾" x 4½ at 213.8 cid
Horsepower:..............80 hp at 3,600 rpm
Weight:..................................... 3,060 lbs
Wheelbase:....................................... 119"
Cost:.......................... $1,100 cut to $925

Production: N/A

Features: It has great horsepower in proportion to its weight. The motor is set low and the engine starter is on the dash.

History: Hudson began their eight-cylinder engines. There were two different chassis lengths. The smaller line was the Model T, and the longer chassis line was the Model U. Roy D. Chapin, Hudson's chairman of the board, became the chairman of the Sixth International Road Conference. Roy D. Chapin was made an officer of the Legion of Honor by the French government, in recognition of his services.

Context: Pluto, the ninth planet, is discovered by astronomers. In American art, Grant Wood paints American Gothic. President Herbert Hoover signs the Hawley-Smoot Tariff Act, weakening the already failing global economy. Over 1,300 American banks fail and unemployment exceeds four million as the Depression sinks lower.

We purchased this Hudson 8 Model T Coupe with a rumble seat at a car auction at the Elkhart County Fairgrounds east of Goshen, Indiana, on August 11, 2001. The Coupe was owned by Lester Flanigan. He restored it after purchasing it from Richard George of Midvale, Utah, on September 18, 1996. Lester Flanigan lived in Sycamore, Illinois. His son came to Jayco in Middlebury, Indiana, to pick up a trailer he had sold as a dealer. At Jayco they told him about the auto sale being held at the Goshen Fairgrounds. He went back and told his father who was trying to sell the Hudson Coupe without success and convinced him to let him bring the car to the Goshen Auction. I was told of the car being there so went looking and added it to our collection.

1930 Hudson Model: Four-Door Sedan Brougham

Engine:.............................. Eight-cylinder
Engine Size:........2¾" x 4½" for 213.8 cid
Horsepower:...................58 at 3,300 rpm
Weight:..................................... 2,850 lbs
Wheelbase:.......................................129"
Cost:....................... $1,295 cut to $1,194

Production: N/A

Features: The roof is fabric-covered. The Landau arms, which graced the quarters, are also fabric-covered. The radiator filler cap is under the hood. Security nuts and large hubs are on the wire wheels. The Brougham models were built on the 129" Model U chassis only. Hooded doors replaced the louvers on the hood sides.

History: It did not sell well due to its high cost. The Hudson Motor Car Company had a year of contrast. It started out quite well, but ended in losses. These losses were caused by the slump of the Hudson-Essex sales and profits, and the whole industry was severely shaken by the first full year of the Great Depression.

Context: The Nazi party places second in German elections, but Adolf Hitler is kept from his seat in the Reichstag because he is an Austrian citizen. In South Africa, white women can now vote, but blacks are still excluded under the regime that would soon be called Apartheid.

Someone that owned the 1930 Hudson Sedan in the Detroit area had restored this car. He sold it to Don Rettele of Traverse City, Michigan. Don was in the oil drilling business in the local area and had started to collect antique automobiles. He had a steel building erected that could hold more than fifty cars. Don had a heart attack and died young. Ken Hoggard was appointed to oversee the sale of the antique car collection. We heard that a 1930 Hudson Sedan was left in the collection that was restored to first class. We were visiting my wife's parents near Midland, Michigan when I saw the ad in a magazine. The next day we drove to Traverse City to see the car. When the door was opened to see the car, Esta and I had to see it only a few seconds to know that we should own it. We showed this car at many car shows and it always drew a lot of attention. This was the first car we bought in the low 30's.

1931 Hudson Model: T Sports Roadster

```
Engine:.............................. Eight-cylinder
Engine Size:....2-7/8" x 4½" for 233.7 cid
Horsepower:...................87 at 3,600 rpm
Weight:..................................... 2,675 lbs
Wheelbase: ..................................... 119"
Cost:................................................. N/A
```

Production: 12

Features: This custom built car features a boatail body that was popular with Auburn and other cars appealing to sport car enthusiasts.

History: Hudson shipped twelve rolling chassis to the Murray Body Company, that also supplied Model A bodies for Ford, to create this boatail speedster. Only five of these cars survive.

Context: The country was in the depths of the depression. Prohibition and public apathy towards the law gave rise to great profits in bootlegging, and the American gangster was a prominent figure during the 1930s. In spite of the hard economic times, the Empire State Building was dedicated and the George Washington Bridge was completed and opened to the public.

I had seen many pictures of this 1931 Hudson eight-cylinder Boatail Speedster painted yellow and orange that was owned by someone in Wisconsin. I always thought when I saw the photo that I needed to own a car like that made by Murray Body Builders. When we were in Fort Wayne, Indiana, at an antique glass show we stopped at a booth that had many nice pieces of glass. We soon learned that the husband of the lady there was into collecting unusual cars. I asked if he had any Hudsons. She said, "It is funny you should ask. He just purchased a 1931 Hudson Boatail Speedster. It is the only Hudson in his collection." I asked if I could see it since I had never actually seen one. She gave me a phone number to call. I called and then got to see this car with no thought that I could ever own it, but I left word for the owner to give me first chance if he ever wanted to sell it. About a year later Mr. Donald E. Galbreath called me with word that the car was for sale. He said he and a partner were working on a project and after a meeting together he decided he needed to put up or shut up. He was ready to sell three of his best cars so he could put up enough money to remove him from the project. So then I owned this nice green Hudson Boatail Speedster.

1931 Hudson Model: The Greater Hudson

In October of 1994 we went to the Hershey Pennsylvania Antique Car Meet. There was an unusual 1930-1931 combination car for sale there. The dash and steering wheel were 1930 model, but from the cowl forward, including the side mounts, radiator, and hood ornament, it was a 1931 model. The car had no provisions for side curtains. All this made the car an interesting one for me to observe. Also, this car had flag pockets on the front and back bumpers. This had been specially built for someone. Bill Chapin, President of the Hudson motor Car Company, was asked to take the office of Secretary of Commerce, so it seemed natural for him to put together a car like this if President Hoover should ever need a seven passenger car for a special event. We purchased the car and found much more information on the car. An army chaplain brought the car back from Panama where he was stationed. We purchased the car from William T. Gaciouch of Orchard Park, New York, on October 7, 1994. The car was on display in Harrah's Museum for many years and had been sold to Donald Arnett of Long Beach, California, on September 26, 1994. We did a total restoration on the car to put it back to the original colors.

Engine:	Eight-cylinder
Engine Size:	3" x 4½" for 254.4 cid
Horsepower:	110 at 3,600 rpm
Weight:	3,190 lbs
Wheelbase:	127"
Cost:	N/A

Production: 1

Features: This car is considered a 1931 model, although it has some 1930 components.

History: In 1930, President Herbert Hoover appointed Roy D. Chapin, then President of the Hudson Motor Car Company, as the Secretary of Commerce. When Hoover made plans to meet with Latin American leaders in Panama, Chapin offered a special Hudson for the trip. The car was left there after the visit and reportedly used as a taxi for many years and then parked. Subsequently, it was returned to the United States and acquired by Harrah's Museum. The car was purchased in restored condition and added to the Hostetler collection in 1994.

Context: Unemployment was estimated at five million when a bank panic gripped the country. In the midst of the economic difficulties, President Hoover signed the bill making *The Star Spangled Banner* the national anthem.

1932 Hudson Model: Essex Terraplane Convertible

This is a Briggs body Essex Convertible that the Chapin family owned and drove. The three Chapin boys drove this convertible through high school and college. When Roy Chapin passed away in 1936, the car was willed to the Edison Institute in Greenfield Village in Detroit, Michigan. When the Institute was disbanded, Mark Smith from Pennsylvania bought the car and had it for many years. He deals and rotates his cars. Someone told me he would sell the 1932 Essex if he got his price. We purchased the 1932 Essex in August of 1993. He has called me since then, wanting to buy it back, but I told him it is already promised to Shipshewana, Indiana. In 1932 the Essex name was dropped and replaced with Terraplane for the 1933 year models. This was done with big publicity through Amelia Earhart, the airplane pilot.

```
Engine: .................. Six-cylinder Hudson
Engine Size:...2-15/16" x 4¾" for 193 cid
Horsepower:...................70 at 3,200 rpm
Weight:..................................... 2,760 lbs
Wheelbase:......................................113"
Cost:................................................$845
```

Production: Low, only 17,425 Essex cars were built.

Features: Large engine in light short wheelbase car.

History: The Essex Terraplane was offered as a Hudson series in 1932 and then as a separate model in 1933. The first Terraplane was given to Orville Wright and the second to Amelia Earhart. The big engine in a light car produced a fast and nimble automobile that was the choice of John Dillenger and other nefarious characters.

Context: The poor demand for goods and the uncertain financial climate made this one of the most unfavorable business years. The "Hoover salute" became popular during the presidential campaign as the 11 million unemployed often stood with their pockets turned out to greet the campaigning President Hoover and show him they were broke. A riot at the Ford plant left four dead and a hundred wounded. We were singing *"Brother Can You Spare Me a Dime?"*

1933 Hudson Model: Terraplane Convertible

This is a very rare car. We don't know of any other eight cylinder Terraplane convertible with two side mounted tires. Several other eight cylinder convertibles known have one spare in the back. We purchased this car from Albert Muller who lived in Eidson, Tennessee. It was a very interesting location where he lived in the mountains of Tennessee. We were coming down a steep hill and with our truck and trailer we couldn't make the sharp left turn required to go back up a hill road to his place. We went many miles to an abandoned filling station to find room to circle around. We were then able to make the right hand turn to go back up the road. After several miles we came to his mail box. He lived way back off the road up a steep hill. We had to cross a creek that had a culvert with cement ends we needed to cross. The wheels of our trailer ran at the very edge of each side (no room for error in driving)! We made it in and back out without falling into the creek!

Engine:.............................. Eight-cylinder
Engine Size:...2-15/16" x 4½" for 244 cid
Horsepower:...................94 at 3,200 rpm
Weight:..................................... 2,495 lbs
Wheelbase:...................................... 113"
Cost:... $625

Production: Terraplane cars gained in popularity.

Features: It has an adjustable steering post, hydraulic shock absorbers, and motors equipped with thermostats.

History: Roy D. Chapin had been Secretary of Commerce for seven months under President Hoover. In March of 1933, he went back to his duties as chairman of the board of directors. He also took on greater duties as president and general manager in hopes to guide the company out of the depression, but could not prevent another financial loss for the company. The Terraplane did set great records. Beating the old record by 51 seconds was Al Miller. He used a Terraplane Standard Six Roadster. Chet Miller set a record for a trip to the summit of Mount Washington of 13 minutes, 33 seconds. By the end of 1933, the Terraplane held 50 hill-climbing records.

Context: Frequency modulations (FM) permit radio reception without static. President Franklin Roosevelt begins to record his "fireside chats" for weekly radio broadcast.

1933 Hudson Model: Essex Terraplane Flower Car

This car came out of New Jersey originally as a funeral flower car. It was customized with special outside lights and inside paneling when new. The unit was used for many years and then parked until reclaimed. V.C. Cantrell of Annville, Pennsylvania found the truck and brought it back to Pennsylvania to start restoration. He had it in the AACA Show in 1991 at Hershey, Pennsylvania. When I saw it I told him if he should consider selling the 1933 Panel Terraplane he should call me. I gave him my card with my number. In 1992 we took our trailer to Hershey, Pennsylvania and brought back the 1933 Terraplane Panel Truck.

Engine: .... Six-cylinder Terraplane
Engine Size:...N/A
Horsepower:...70
Weight:..N/A
Wheelbase:......................................106"
Cost:......... $440 plus custom body work

Production: N/A

Features: Custom lamps and coach work.

History: The flower car was converted from the Essex Terraplane panel truck with the addition of interior paneling and special coach lamps. This was a transition year for the Essex, when the Terraplane was a model designation and not yet a separate vehicle built by the Hudson Motor Car Company.

Context: The jobless rate had now grown to 15 million, but Henry Ford said, "Times are good! We are in the 'oxcart stage' of the machine age." In fact, Roosevelt's New Deal programs were beginning to create new jobs. The first drive-in movie was built in Camden, New Jersey, and prohibition finally ended. We were singing *"Stormy Weather"* and *"Boulevard of Broken Dreams."*

1935 Hudson Model: Custom Brougham, Series 54

This is a long wheelbase Hudson with an electric hand semi-automatic shifting system. The car had wire wheels with two side mounted spare tires and an eight cylinder L head type motor. The car came out of the Denver, Colorado area. Gus Souza of Chicago, Illinois, had the car for several years. He sold it to Jack Miller in the spring of 1994. We purchased the car from Jack Miller in the fall of 1994.

Engine.....................	Six-cylinder Hudson
Engine Size:.............	3" x 3½" for 254 cid
Horsepower:................	113 at 3,800 rpm
Weight:.....................................	3,055 lbs
Wheelbase:......................................	118"
Cost:..	$1,025

Production: N/A

Features: This car has the new electric hand shifter, twin horns, and twin side-mounts.

History: This car was sold originally in Lancaster, Pennsylvania for $1,168, and was chauffeur driven. Hudson set seven new records at Daytona, including a top speed of 88.051 mph, and 36 new speed records at Muroc Lake, California, in 1935. This car is unrestored and was added to the Hostetler collection in 1994.

Context: It was the year of the great dust storms over Texas, Kansas, and Oklahoma and hordes of people migrated to California, living out of beat-up jalopies and seeking relief. President Franklin Roosevelt signed the Social Security Act.

1936 Hudson Model: Convertible Coupe with Rumble Seat, Series 65

This car was purchased in Arizona by Phil J. Kuhn in 1971. He added several things to the car during the years he owned it. I talked to him several times about buying the 1936 convertible. He always said he was not ready yet to sell. About a year after the last time he called me and said it was for sale because he needed to cut back in his work. We managed to get together on a price; then we owned a special 1936 convertible car. This car has all the extras that Hudson had for any car. To start with there is a rumble seat, electric-hand, twin side mounts, twin spot lights, twin fog lights, twin fender lights, fender skirts, large wheel covers, radio, clock, motor light and twin wig-wag lights.

Engine:	Eight-cylinder
Engine Size:	3" x 4½" for 254 cid
Horsepower:	113 at 3,800 rpm
Weight:	3,000 lbs
Wheelbase:	120"
Cost:	$895

Production: N/A, but limited.

Features: This beautifully restored car offers electric hand transmission, dual side mounts, and rear fender skirts, large hubcaps, twin fog lamps, dual spot lights, fender parking lamps, radio, clock and dual wig-wag stop lights. Note the suicide doors (they open from the front).

History: The car was purchased in 1994 and restored in 1995.

Context: Franklin D. Roosevelt's New Deal increased the national debt to $12 billion, but at the same time increased national income to $30 billion. The Hindenburg completed its first scheduled transatlantic flight and the Queen Mary landed in New York City. Movies were very popular and we were watching Charlie Chaplin in *"Modern Times"* at the local Bijou.

1936 Hudson Model: Touring Sedan, Series 67

Engine:................Eight-cylinder Hudson
Engine Size:............3" x 4½" for 254 cid
Horsepower:................134 at 3,800 rpm
Weight:....................................3,140 lbs
Wheelbase:.....................................124"
Cost:..$975

Production: N/A

Features: Dual side mounts, dual horns, and fender skirts.

History: The new styling motif for 1936 was attractive and the company offered improved steering and better braking. Hudson shipped 25,409 cars to dealers and declared a profit of $3.3 million.

Context: Franklin D. Roosevelt was elected president for a second term and the economy was on the rise with improved farm prices and a 20% increase in automobile production. The age of the automobile trailer reached new heights with a reported 160,000 on the road. Economic times were still tough in this country with eight million unemployed and *"Pennies from Heaven"* was a popular song at the time. The first Social Security checks were mailed to retired citizens and the winds of war began to blow in Europe as the German army marched into the Rhineland.

This is a long wheelbase car that was found in a junk yard in Stevens Point, Wisconsin. The person that retrieved the car had intentions of restoring it when he got the car in 1957. He never got started restoring it so in 1987 he sold this car to George Nels of Hubertus, Wisconsin. He started on a total restoration of this 1936 Hudson. He wasn't done when his health began to deteriorate so we bought the car and finished the restoration with new upholstery and detailing the motor compartment.

1937 Hudson Model: Terraplane Four-Door Sedan, Bubble Trunk

```
Engine:................................. Six-cylinder
Engine Size:.......... 3 x 4½" for 254.4 cid
Horsepower:.................102 at 3,900 rpm
Weight:......................................3,135 lbs
Wheelbase:.........................................122"
Cost:...................................................$865
```

Production: Total Terraplane passenger cars was 83,436.

Features: It was a very fast automobile. This model has been altered with the addition of the steering post shift lever (This was not standard on Hudson cars until 1939).

History: The 1,000 mile AAA record for closed cars of unlimited (size or price) class was broken in 1937. The Terraplane averaged 86.54 mph and 21.08 miles per gallon. Many other records were also set. In addition, seven new Class C marks were credited to the Terraplane. The end of the year was shadowed by the accidental death of Howard E. Coffin, a very noted engineer at the Hudson Motor Car Company. As he prepared for the opening of the hunting season at his home, an accidental rifle shot took his life.

Context: Amelia Earhart and her aircraft disappear mysteriously over the Pacific Ocean. One of the most influential architects of the twentieth century, Frank Lloyd Wright, completes Falling Water in Bear Rock, Pennsylvania.

We purchased this 1937 Hudson Terraplane Sedan at a car sales lot in Mishawaka, Indiana. The car was placed there by Robert F. Wright of Ohio. K.M. Gillies was the car sales lot owner and a relative of the car owner. When I saw the Hudson Terraplane with a "For Sale" tag in the window, I stopped, investigated the car, and took a test drive. He had many extra parts available to go with the car. We thought the car was worth the asking price so we purchased it on September 16, 1985. It was one of the early cars starting our large Hudson car collection.

1937 Hudson Model: Custom Eight, Series 77

Engine:	Eight-cylinder
Engine Size:	3" x 4½" for 254 cid
Horsepower:	122 at 4,200 rpm
Weight:	3,195 lbs
Wheelbase:	129"
Cost:	$965

Production: N/A, annual production of all cars was less than 20,000.

Features: Hydraulic brakes on all four wheels and hydraulic hill holder.

History: Hudson broke all existing class C speed records for closed stock cars from ten to 2,000 miles and speed and endurance records from one to 24 hours. A Hudson Eight Deluxe Brougham covered 2,104.22 miles in 24 hours at an average speed of 87.67 mph. Hudson shipped only 19,848 cars this year.

Context: Economic unrest was prevalent. There were labor revolts and strikes at Ford, General Motors, and Chrysler, as well as in the coal mines in West Virginia, at the steel mills in Youngstown, Ohio, and by the screen actors in Hollywood. The grand Hindenburg dirigible exploded as it tried to dock at Lakeland, New Jersey. Walt Disney's *"Snow White and the Seven Dwarfs"* was a grand hit at the local Bijou theater.

This car was found in the basement of a home in Lynbrook, New York. The car was owned by a doctor. The original sale bill shows that he paid $1,289.81 for the car. It is a long wheelbase Hudson Sedan with a tray in the back of the front seat. The car was advertised in a car magazine. It had been purchased at an estate auction and placed on the market by Roy's Auto Sales of South Hampton, New Hampshire. The car had only 16,000 miles on it. We purchased the car in July of 1994. We had to redo the inside upholstery due to moth damage. This is an excellent low mileage car.

1937 Railton, with a Hudson Eight-Cylinder Chassis

Engine:................................ Eight-cylinder
Engine Size:.............. 3" x 4½" at 254 cid
Horsepower:.. N/A
Weight:.. N/A
Wheelbase:...................................... 120"
Cost:.. N/A

Production: N/A

Features: New styling forms were adopted in the form of flowing lines, curves, contours, and domed-shaped, giving an inflated appearance.

History: Roy D. Chapin died of pneumonia just before his 56th birthday. Hudson Motor Car Company's position as one of the leading auto companies is attributed to him. Railton, a distributor of Hudson cars in England, was shipped an eight-cyclinder Hudson chassis. Ranalah Coachworks of Wimble, England, made the convertible coupe body which also included a rumble seat. Two seats are also located behind the front seat facing each other. The distributor, Railton, placed his own name on the coupe. The CCCA and AACA clubs both consider all the Railton cars as classic.

Context: In baseball, Joe DiMaggio joins the New York Yankees, who win the World Series, 4-2, against the New York Giants. Franklin Delano Roosevelt is re-elected President.

Pete Booz of California called me saying his wife had filed for divorce. He needed to quickly raise some money to settle things. He asked if I would be interested in his 1937 Railton with a Hudson chassis under it. It had an eight cylinder motor in a convertible model with a rumble seat and two rear facing child seats in back of the front seat. My first impulse was to think that the cost would be way beyond my means. The car was made in Cabham, England, by Ranalah Coachworks. Only four of these models were ever made. Hudson Motors sold their chassis to many custom body companies. In 1997 Pete Booz bought the car from Ray Pschirer in Pennsylvania. We purchased it from Pete Booz in September of 2003.

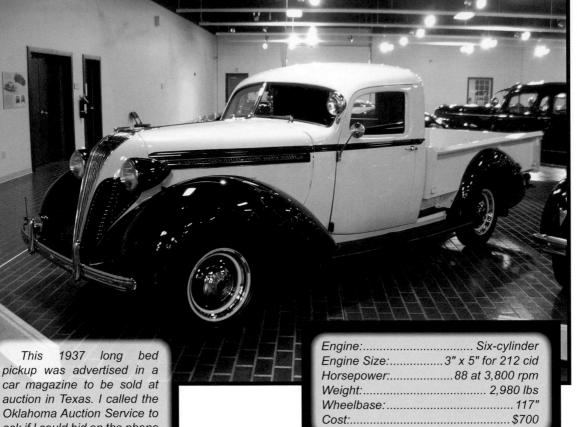

1937 Hudson Model: Terraplane Pickup Express, Series 70

Engine:................................. Six-cylinder
Engine Size:...............3" x 5" for 212 cid
Horsepower:...................88 at 3,800 rpm
Weight:...................................... 2,980 lbs
Wheelbase:....................................... 117"
Cost:... $700

This 1937 long bed pickup was advertised in a car magazine to be sold at auction in Texas. I called the Oklahoma Auction Service to ask if I could bid on the phone for the 1937 Terraplane Pickup. He assured me I could and told me how it would happen. This is the only Hudson I ever bought "sight unseen" and it taught me a lesson. I was told this was a nice brown colored pickup. When it was unloaded I fully understood what the term "Beauty is in the eye of the beholder" meant! It was the ugliest brown color I could ever think of. I was sure this pickup could never be shown before it was restored. The pickup was purchased on April 7, 1986, and when the restoration was completed it turned out to be a very good pickup to show, and got great remarks.

Production: Approximately 7,000 commercial 70 series vehicles of all kinds.

Features: The tri-color paint, side mounts and art deco style, make this one of the most attractive trucks of the decade.

History: These trucks were very popular because they offered a bed that would hold a 4' x 8' sheet of plywood, which Ford and Chevrolet did not offer until 1953. The truck was purchased for the collection in 1986.

Context: While the worst of the Great Depression was over, economic unrest was prevalent with a large number of sit-down strikes. The government claimed that these strikes involved over half a million workers. Construction projects continued, however, as the Lincoln Tunnel was completed and the Golden Gate Bridge was dedicated.

1938 Hudson Model: Country Club Sedan Four-Door

Engine:............................. Eight-cylinder	
Engine Size:...........3" x 4½" at 254.4 cid	
Horsepower:................122 at 4,200 rpm	
Weight:..................................... 3,270 lbs	
Wheelbase:.......................................129"	
Cost:...$1,219	

We knew about this car located in Denver, Colorado, for twenty years. It was owned by the Soneff Brothers, antique car dealers in Denver. We stopped at their place whenever we were in the area. John always had new things that he was promoting. I would ask when he was going to let me buy the 1938 Hudson Country Club Sedan. John and his brother could never agree when that would be. However, John placed an ad stating the car was going to be auctioned in May of 2006. I called to ask why he hadn't let me know the car was for sale. His response was that he wanted to put it on the sale with a reserve bid. If it brought the reserve he would let it go. He asked if I could come and bid on it. I told him I would pay the reserve bid and felt he should let me have it to complete my collection. John told me he would call me back after talking with his brother. In May of 2006, before the auction, John called and said I could have the car. The first car I had owned was a standard 1938 four-door sedan with an electric-hand semi-automatic shifting system made by Bendix of South Bend, Indiana. Since this car also had all of these extras and was still working, I was glad to get this special car!

Production: N/A

Features: These cars were the heaviest and highest-priced Hudsons offered in America. They also had the longest chassis. This particular car has all the extra options that were available in 1938 such as the semi-automatic shifting system, which still works.

History: A record was set at the Hudson Motor Company this year. They offered 56 passenger cars and 16 utility and commercial models. Roy D. Chapin, Jr., the son of the founder, joined the Hudson Motor Company, and began work in the engineering department. This vehicle was purchased in 2006 for the Hostetler collection.

Context: Congress passes the Fair Labor Standards Act, providing a minimum wage for the first time. In the radio broadcast "War of the Worlds", Orson Welles panics Americans who believe that Martians are actually invading Earth. The first real "Xerox" image is made in the borough of Queens, New York. "Snow White and the Seven Dwarfs" is Walt Disney's first full-length animated film.

1940 Hudson Model: Traveler Business Coupe, Series 40T

In February of 1992 we purchased this utility coupe from John D. Lebold of Perrysburg, Ohio. He had totally restored the coupe. I had seen this coupe at the AACA Show in Hershey, Pennsylvania several years earlier. I had told him if he ever thought of selling this car he should give me a call. I gave him one of my cards. He had won a number of trophies with this one-of-a-kind car. The box is on rollers and pulls out of the trunk; the box can go back in and you then close the trunk lid. It is sort of a truck / coupe type of car. Salesmen were encouraged to use it to haul samples in sales work. The Hudson Motor Car Company made this available from 1935 to 1942.

Engine:................................. Six-cylinder
Engine Size:........3" x 4-1/8" at 174.9 cid
Horsepower:...................92 at 4,000 rpm
Weight:...................................... 2,890 lbs
Wheelbase:...................................... 113"
Cost:.. $672

Production: Less than 1,000.

Features: A small truck body slides out from the trunk of the Business Coupe, so that the car served as both passenger car and small cargo carrier.

History: Company production fell to tenth in the industry with a loss of $1.5 million for the year.

Context: The 40-hour work week was sanctioned, and unemployment dropped dramatically due to military conscription and increase in productivity to meet the demands of the war in Europe. The US was producing large amounts of material for Great Britain. Germany conquered the Netherlands, Denmark, Belgium, and France. We were singing *"When You Wish Upon a Star"* and *"You Are My Sunshine."*

1942 Hudson Model: Wood-Bodied Station Wagon, Series 21

After we had all the cars listed to be shown in the museum, someone asked if the left over wood could be wired together to make it look like it was when it was bought. I contacted Jan Appenzeller to see if he would attempt this. He said he had also thought this should be done so it could be parked next to the restored car. He came and wired the wood together to show how bad it had been to start with!

Engine:...........................Six-cylinder	
Engine Size:.........3" x 5" for 212 cid	
Horsepower:...........102 at 4,000 rpm	
Weight:...............................3,315 lbs	
Wheelbase:...............................121"	
Cost:..$1,486	

A bear hunter reported to a Hudson club member that a 1942 Hudson Woodie Wagon with a Campbell body tag was sitting on a mountain top at the north edge of Death Valley. This started all kinds of talk because Hudson only sold Woodie Wagons made by Cantrell Woodie Company. After much talk Pete Booz and his wife went looking. The mountain was so steep they had to crawl on hands and knees to get there and spent most of a day to get up there and back. Upon closer inspection it was determined that it sure was a Campbell made Woodie! There was no motor, no radiator, and no drive train on this Woodie. It was rigged to be pulled up and down behind a crawler tractor to take mined minerals down in plastic tubs and supplies back up. The Woodie was brought out by Carl Mendosa who restored Woodies for the surf riders of San Diego, California. He sold this Woodie to Richard Griffin to be restored. Richard brought it to Al Saffrahn of Phoenix, Arizona, for help in getting it done. My son, Eldon Jr., lived in Arizona so we went to Al Saffrahn's place. Al worked on Hudsons and there sat this Woodie in need of much help. He told us it was for sale because he couldn't think of trying to restore the Woodie. I measured the wheelbase and came back home and checked magazines for a long wheelbase Hudson Sedan. We found one at a farm sale near Staunton, Virginia, which we purchased. The Woodie was then purchased and Wooden Naga, Inc. of LaPorte, Indiana, did the replacement wood. The Appenzeller Brothers did the rest of the restoration. It turned out great and is a very interesting Woodie.

Production: N/A

Features: The original wood body was by the Campbell Body Works of Watertown, New York, distinguished by the wood sides covering the running boards.

History: This car was found by chance on a mountain top 7,000 feet above Death Valley. It took a bulldozer to open a path and bring it down. The car needed a new chassis and drive train which were later found at an auction. It took five years to fabricate the replacement wood pieces and another year to put the car together. Restoration was completed in 1999.

Context: The war time phrase, "Praise the Lord and pass the ammunition," was first uttered by a Chaplin on the New Orleans during the Pearl Harbor attack. America was at war; steel, gas, tires, sugar and butter were rationed. The sale of new cars and trucks was banned on January 1, 1942.

1946 Hudson Model: Super-Six Brougham Convertible, Series 51

Engine:............................. Eight-cylinder
Engine Size:................................ 254 cid
Horsepower:................. 198 at 4,000 rpm
Weight:..................................... 3,195 lbs
Wheelbase:......................................121"
Cost:..$2,050

Production: Approximately 140.

Features: The engine block is chrome alloy and is so hard that it is very difficult to machine. This car includes an overdrive transmission.

History: These cars were built late in the production year to stimulate sales. Construction started by removing the top from a coupe and then adding the canvas top.

Context: The war was over, but peace-time America seemed to be encircled by one giant picket line from the auto industry to the steel mills, the shipping docks, and taxi drivers. Reportedly, New Yorkers were eating horse meat because of food shortages. The repeal of L85 legislation that regulated women's skirt length during the war lead to the lowering of hemlines and a clothing purchase frenzy by style conscious women. We were watching *"The Best Years of our Lives"* at the Bijou theater and singing *"Zip-a-dee-doo-dah."*

Right after the war in 1946, Hudson Motor Car Company was not going to make any convertibles. Toward the end of the year, many southern states dealers wanted convertibles to sell. The decision was made to pull one hundred coupe bodies off the lines, cut the tops off, and reinforce the under carriage so as to support the body without a metal top. Hudson made cars under the names Super-Six, Commodore Six, and Commodore Eight. They made them into three categories and only thirty-some of each kind were ever made. We were able to find a Commodore Eight for sale in Hepburn, Saskatchewan, Canada, in 1990. We purchased it and restored the car in 1993. It is one of only a few left.

1947 Hudson Model: Super-Six, Two-Door

Engine:................................. Six-cylinder
Engine Size:................3" x 5" for 212 cid
Horsepower:....................................... 102
Weight:..................................... 3,055 lbs
Wheelbase:.....................................121"
Cost:... $1,704

Production: N/A

Features: The front medallion was in a new die-casting which had a flared edge. The Hudson nameplate was now put on the trunk lid. Also, there was a key lock fitted to the driver's door.

History: A vice-presidency of sales was created. The office was given to George H. Pratt. This is the last year that Hudson made a frame that was made separately from the body of the car.

Context: Dr. Edwin H. Land introduces a new camera that can produce a developed photographic image in sixty seconds. Jackie Robinson joins the Brooklyn Dodgers becoming the first black man to play in baseball's Major Leagues. The National Security Act creates both the Defense Department and the Central Intelligence Agency. Archaeologists decipher the law code of Hammurabi. A young boy finds the Dead Sea Scrolls near Qumran.

In 1987 Mike Whited of Perry, Michigan, said he would sell his Hudson coach. He had the car repainted black, but the upholstery needed to be redone. We didn't do much of anything to this car since purchasing the car since it always looked nice from the outside. This car has an unusual pivot to the front seat to get into the back seat. This was the last year that Hudson made cars where the body was separate from the frame.

Engine.................................	Six-cylinder
Engine Size:.............3" x 4½" for 254 cid	
Horsepower:.. 102	
Weight:..................................... 3,500 lbs	
Wheelbase:.....................................128"	
Cost:...$1,675	

Production: 2,917

Features: Running boards were sturdy and exposed, and had a ¾ ton pay load. A spacious cab which could hold three large men easily, and a large rear window and windshield for safety and comfort were also great features. Among some of the options was the new Hudson Weather-master, a car air-conditioning system.

History: The Cab Pickup was Hudson's last entry in the commercial vehicle market.

Context: The Truman Doctrine establishes the American cold war policy, "Containment." Also announced this year, the Marshall Plan will direct massive funds to assist European economic recovery. In Long Island, New York, builders erect Levittown, a middle-class suburb; by 1970 more Americans will live in the suburbs than in cities. The United State's Gross National Product begins its historic postwar surge, ushering in an era of economic growth.

This was the last year Hudson Motor Car Company made any pickup trucks. They had two models: a one-half ton and a three-quarter ton pickup. The one we purchased was a Long Boy three-quarter ton. We had a phone call from Elkhart, Indiana, that a family had moved from Michigan to Elkhart and used the truck to move and now wanted to sell it. The wife inherited the truck from her father when he died the previous year. She had grown up on a farm where this truck was used a lot. The father restored the truck before his death for the daughter's use. We purchased this truck in 2001. We spent money to restore the truck bed.

1948 Hudson Model: Four-Door, Super-Six

```
Engine:.................................. Six-cylinder
Engine Size:. 3-9/16" x 4-3/8" for 262 cid
Horsepower:.................128 at 4,000 rpm
Weight:...................................... 3,500 lbs
Wheelbase:......................................124"
Cost:............................................$2,222
```

We purchased several cars from Mike Whited of Perry, Michigan, in 1987. This car came close to one I had during the time I bought and drove Hudson cars doing sales and service work. I had a 1950 Commodore Eight with all the options available for the gold colored 1950 with gold upholstery and the motor set up with high compression for fast driving on the highway. There were no speed limits then.

Production: Approximately 50,000 Super-Six Hudsons of all styles were built.

Features: The step down design, in which the car was built between the frame rather than on top of it. All modern cars are built in this manner.

History: The new body style was created by a group of designers under the direction of Fran Spring and was used in New York City in one of the first TV advertising campaigns.

Context: World War II was behind us and the first true new car models since 1942 were introduced to the public. Wages at General Motors and Chrysler were increased to $1.61 an hour to settle a strike. The controversial Tucker was introduced, but was pummeled by legal and political events, limiting total production to 50 automobiles. We were watching *"South Pacific"* on Broadway and singing *"All I Want for Christmas is My Two Front Teeth."*

1951 Hudson Model: Brougham Convertible, Parade Car

Engine.............................. *Eight-cylinder*
Engine Size:............. *3" x 4½" for 254 cid*
Horsepower:.. *N/A*
Weight:..................................... *3,800 lbs*
Wheelbase:...................................... *124"*
Cost:... *$3,099*

This car was purchased at the Kruse Auction in 1991. The car was customized by a restoration shop located in Oklahoma for a movie. We were told the car was used in two movies and then sold. The movies they said it had been used in have never been found by anyone. I bought the car because it is a great parade car!

Production: There was a total production run of 14,243 in the four models of the Commodore Custom Eight Series.

Features: An optional transmission was offered. It was the four-speed Hydra-Matic Drive of General Motors. Also available was Hudson's own Drive-Master (without overdrive).

History: To handle defense contracts because of the Korean situation, Hudson offices in Washington D.C. were established. They had contracts for Wright aircraft engine parts, rear fuselage, and tail sections for B-57 Canberra bombers, and Boeing Statojet bombers. The Hostetler collection purchased this car in 1991.

Context: Julius and Ethel Rosenberg, accused of cold war espionage, are sentenced to death. The Rosenbergs are executed in 1953 amid protest. One of the greats in baseball history, Mickey Mantle, joins the New York Yankees, who win the World Series this year, 4-2. The musical *"The King and I"* by Richard Rodgers and Oscar Hammerstein, hits Broadway. U.S. surgeon John Gibbon Jr. creates the first heart-lung machine.

1951 Hudson Model: Convertible

Engine:................................ Six-cylinder
Engine Size:...3-13/16" x 4½" for 308 cid
Horsepower:................145 at 3,800 rpm
Weight:...................................... 3,780 lbs
Wheelbase:....................................... 119"
Cost:..$3,099

This car was purchased in 1987 in the northern suburbs of New York City. This was the first year the Hudson Motor Car Company offered Twin-H-Power for 308 cubic inch displacement motors. This was the first muscle car available in the automobile world. Hudson never got any credit for offering it to the public. The setup consisted of a special intake manifold that had two carburetors on a six cylinder motor. The stock car racers were able to buy this setup in 1950 and install it on their race cars. This is why Hudson cars won almost all stock car races from 1950 to 1954. We have shown our restored 1951 Hudson at many car shows where it almost always wins People's Choice Award, but not often do Hudsons win any judging awards. The self-appointed car experts never did like the Hudson Motor Car Company products. I experienced this the first time I entered my 1911 Hudson Race Car at the Meadowbrook Show in Rochester, Michigan. I was placed with Cadillac and others of the same year in a circle. Three judges spent quite some time judging the Cadillac. (We were asked to sit behind the car and answer any questions the judges might care to ask.) The judge checking the undercarriage of the Cadillac was done first and his remark was that an interesting car was coming up next as he was looking at the side of my Speedster saying it was either a Stutz or a Marmon Racer. He walked in front of my car and saw the Hudson name and said, "It's only a Hudson" making one trip around it and left. So did the other two judges. I knew then that Hudson was not accepted.

Production: 550

Features: High performance engine, twin power with dual carburetors.

History: The company lost $1.5 million this year on sales of 131,915 vehicles They were ranked 15th in the industry. It was the first year of the twin power engine with dual carburetors and Hudson won 12 of 41 NASCAR events with this setup that year. Restoration was completed in 1988.

Context: The world teetered on the brink of World War III and General Douglas MacArthur, a hero of World War II, retired from service with the quote, "Old soldiers never die, they just fade away." Inflation was rampant and 200,000 items, including automobiles, were placed under price controls. TV was becoming a dominant feature of our lives, and the first color TV broadcast was presented by Columbia Broadcasting. We were watching Humphrey Bogart in *"The African Queen"* at the local cinema and singing *"Hello Young Lovers."*

1953 Hudson Model: Super Wasp Hollywood

Engine.................................	Six-cylinder
Engine Size:. 3-9/16" x 4-3/8" for 262 cid	
Horsepower:.....................................	127
Weight:....................................	3,525 lbs
Wheelbase:....................................	119"
Cost:...	$2,812

Production: The Wasp and the Super Wasp were combined and had a total production of 17,792.

Features: A "Step-Down" designed Monobuilt body and frame. It also had Center-Point Steering and specially selected alloy steel which provided independent front-wheel coil springing for a smoother ride.

History: The Jet car was produced during the year, but it did not do well. Its cost was too high for its size, and the styling was not attractive to buyers. This Super Wasp Hollywood was purchased by the Hostetler collection in 1997 to replace a 1953 Hudson Wasp, four-door, sedan which had been totaled. The engine and drive train were removed from the sedan and placed in the Hollywood because it was bought without an engine. The sedan had less than 30,000 miles on it. The restoration was completed in June of 1998 by the Appenzeller Brothers, Pat and Jan.

Context: Josip Tito becomes president of liberal Communist state Yugoslavia. Francis Crick and James Watson discover the "double helix" of DNA.

I had purchased a four-door Hudson at the Kruse Auction on September 9, 1994. We had it several years when it became involved in a serious accident that nearly killed me. On June 10, 1997, while making a left turn into my driveway, I was hit at the driver's door of the car hard enough to bend the car enough for both back windows to break out. The car was totaled out. I found a Hollywood Wasp in Littleton, Colorado that had no motor or right front fender and purchased that car. We put the motor of the wrecked car into it and the drive train from that car because of the low mileage as well as the right front fender. At Hershey I found a Twin-H-Power setup for the Wasp and so we then had a complete car. The Hollywood originally had a factory installed vinyl head liner which is something we had never seen in a Wasp car.

1954 Hudson Model: Hornet Four-Door, Twin-H Four

Engine:.................................	Six-cylinder
Engine Size:...3-13/16" x 4½" for 308 cid	
Horsepower:......................................	170
Weight:......................................	3,620 lbs
Wheelbase:.......................................	124"
Cost:...	$2,769

Production: N/A

Features: There was a provision for recessed back-up lights because massive chrome stretched across the rear which was above the bumper. This Hornet has Twin-H-Power.

History: Hudson and Nash-Kalvinator merged to become American Motors Corporation. George Mason, chairman of the board of directors, who founded the above mentioned, suddenly died. George W. Romney, executive vice-president, took over Mason's responsibilities. This Hornet was purchased for the Hostetler collection in 2005. It has its original paint color which is "Lipstick Red". This is very special because during the last week of car production in Detroit, Michigan, this is the final color used.

Context: Senator Joseph McCarthy accelerates his anti-Communist witch hunt with the nationally televised Army-McCarthy Hearings and is formally censured by Congress. Elvis Presley records *"That's All Right, Mama"* and several other singles.

This Hornet Twin-H-Power is special because it was made the last week of Hudson Car production in Detroit, Michigan. They had much lipstick red paint left that week so all cars were painted that color to use up the paint. This is one of those cars. The car was owned by William Dely of Lewiston, Michigan, who owned it for many years. He never drove it in the winter and had good storage for it. When I saw his ad I called him about the car. He lived near the Mackinaw Bridge. I bought the car in 2005 and put new upholstery in because of moth eaten holes.

1954 Hudson Model: Hudson Jet

We purchased this car from Mike Whited who lived in Perry, Michigan, in 1987. This is an unrestored original car. It has had some damage from moth's eating in the upholstery. The Hudson Motor Car Company tried to introduce a smaller car in 1952, but sales never equalled the cost of getting it into production. This was one thing that Hudson management did that added to its failure in 1954.

Engine.................................. Six-cylinder
Engine Size:..L-head, 3"x4¾" for 202 cid
Horsepower:................ 104 at 4,000 rpm
Weight:..................................... 2,750 lbs
Wheelbase:....................................... N/A
Cost:.. $2,057

Production: 14,224 for all models this year.

Features: This car is an unrestored original. It is well built, but not inexpensive compared to full size vehicles. Note its stainless steel grill.

History: The Jet was not well accepted by the public and did not sell well.

Context: Hurricanes Carol, Edna, and Hazel resulted in property losses of over $650 million. The nation was in a business recession and the automotive industry was in transition. Hudson and Nash-Kalvinator approved a merger to form American Motors while Packard and Studebaker merged in a vain attempt to compete with the big three auto makers: GM, Ford, and Chrysler. Joe DiMaggio married Marilyn Monroe and Frank Sinatra won an Oscar for *"From Here to Eternity."* The number of TV stations reached 360. We were watching *"Rear Window"* and *"On The Water Front"* at the Bijou theater and singing *"Stranger in Paradise"* and *"I Love Paris"*.

1956 Hudson Model: Hornet Sedan

Engine:.................................	Six-cylinder
Engine Size:..................	L-head 3" x 4¾"
Horsepower:.................	120 at 4,000 rpm
Weight:......................................	3,264 lbs
Wheelbase:	N/A
Cost:...	$2,416

On June 22, 1996, I went to a public auction in Greensburg, Pennsylvania that had listed a black and white 1956 Hudson with a Twin-H-Power Hudson motor. This was the last year such a car was made. I took along a letter to prove my ability to pay if I should be able to purchase the car. This is a Nash body with a Hudson motor installed. The car had only 9,936 miles on the odometer and they claimed that to be correct. The car sat in an estate deal for many years and not driven. American Motors stopped making big cars and only made Ramblers after 1957. With some of the profits on Rambler sales they purchased the Jeep which is still popular. Chrysler purchased American Motors which was again purchased by Mercedes Benz of Germany. So this kind of merger will keep going on into the future.

Production: 2,519 before production of the Hudson ceased in 1957.

Features: This car has a six-cylinder engine with Twin H power (dual carburetors). It is an original car with less than 10,000 miles. The front seat reclines, one of the first cars to offer such an option.

History: After Hudson and Nash merged in 1953 to form American Motors, the Hudson name-plate was dropped in 1957 and the company concentrated on the Rambler.

Context: Tension with the USSR dominated foreign policy and social unrest dominated domestic activity. Automobile production was up and 12% of the cars sold were station wagons. President Eisenhower signed the interstate highway bill and the suburban housing boom was underway. We were watching *"The Man with the Golden Arm"* with Frank Sinatra and *"And God Created Woman"* with Brigitte Bardot at the Bijou. We were signing *"Blue Suede Shoes"* and *"On the Street Where You Live"*.